SOCIAL PSYCHOLOGY
OF ABSENTEEISM

SOCIAL PSYCHOLOGY OF ABSENTEEISM

J. K. Chadwick-Jones, Nigel Nicholson and Colin Brown

PRAEGER

PRAEGER SPECIAL STUDIES • PRAEGER SCIENTIFIC

Library of Congress Cataloging in Publication Data

Chadwick-Jones, J. K. (John K.)
  Social psychology of absenteeism.

  Bibliography: p.
  Includes index.
  1. Absenteeism (Labor)—United States.
I. Nicholson, Nigel. II. Brown, Colin, 1945-
III. Title.
HD5115.2.U5C47   306'.3   81-23395
ISBN 0-03-056652-5   AACR2

Published in 1982 by Praeger Publishers
CBS Educational and Professional Publishing
a Division of CBS Inc.
521 Fifth Avenue, New York, New York 10175 U.S.A.

3456789   052   98765432

Printed in the United States of America

To
Araceli, Mary, and Shirley

CONTENTS

ACKNOWLEDGMENTS

Our industrial investigations of 16 organizations, starting in the early 1970s, were carried out with the financial aid of the Department of Employment in England. The research studies in Canada (with Araceli Carceller) and the review publication *Absenteeism in the Canadian Context* (1980) were supported by grants from Canada Labour. In 1978 and 1979 field studies were carried out in three banks, and in 1980–81 research was undertaken in two hospitals. The book was developed from these cumulative investigations in 21 organizations.

Araceli Carceller also worked on the treatment of the Canadian data with the Cambridge (England) IBM 370/165 and took responsibility for all the graphs and figures in the book.

I am grateful to the Canada Social Sciences and Humanities Research Council and to Saint Mary's University, Halifax, Canada, for providing the opportunity to complete the book during a sabbatical year in England.

During this year it has been very pleasant to be a member of the Senior Common Room at St. Edmund Hall in the University of Oxford and to work in association with Arthur Marsh, Senior Fellow of the college.

Occasionally I visited Donald Broadbent at the Department of Experimental Psychology, University of Oxford; these visits provided useful opportunities to discuss the theory and results of the study.

In Cambridge, where I spent the remainder of the year, Colin Fraser, Fellow of Churchill College, was a frequent companion, host, and discussant of absenteeism questions. Cathy Marsh, Fellow of Newnham College, and David Ingleby, Fellow of Darwin College, were helpful and hospitable.

Typing of the many drafts, perhaps four or five for each chapter before this present version appeared, has been done by Rosemary Lewis. Our heartfelt thanks are due to her.

J. K. Chadwick-Jones
Darwin College
University of Cambridge

LIST OF TABLES

LIST OF FIGURES

1

INTRODUCTION

INITIAL PROBLEMS

Studies of absence from work have little to offer in the form of an explanatory framework. In our review of over 100 studies (Chadwick-Jones, Brown, and Nicholson 1973a), we found a variety of methods and approaches. In these studies "absence" had no uniform operational definition: the term referred to sickness absence, to absence for causes unknown, to "certificated" or "uncertificated" absences. No standard approach was found; no normative information was available about attendance (or absence), whether considered as an act of choice or as habitual, routine, or rule-following behavior.

Attempts to examine the etiology of nonsickness absence have been few and inconclusive. While sickness absence has been thoroughly studied by medical researchers, there are relatively few studies (and no large-scale ones) available of absence as the important behavioral phenomenon that some consider it to be (Vroom 1964).

Absence from work, where work is defined by the employee's presence at a particular location (office or workshop) for a fixed period each day, can be interpreted as an individual act of choice between alternative activities; as withdrawal or escape from surveillance; as individual and group resistance to an inflexible system. Thus, absence may also be viewed as a stratagem in intergroup relations, as a defensive or aggressive act in intergroup conflict. On the one hand "absenteeism" may be a pejorative term used by employers; on the other, employees may feel that they have the right to a few days off as part of their (unwritten) work contract.

Thus, there is no consensus about the meaning or nature of absence from work. Even in the reports on sickness absence, we are presented with speculations about malingering and about the use of certificated absence as a conventional means of securing time off for other activities. Physicians have little or no

1

control over certification since, it is estimated, in a large proportion of instances certificates for illness must be given without apparent symptoms, on the patient's word alone (Industrial Society Conference: "Sickness Absence Control," London, 1968).*

In addition to such empirical difficulties, there is a lack of systematic attempts at explanation. Nor is there an overall framework, methodological or theoretical, shared by researchers. Where absence has attracted attention from psychologists, it has usually been treated as a somewhat peripheral index—hypothetically, as an expression of morale or job satisfactions and incidental to these main topics of inquiry. It is often suggested that absences are an expression of job dissatisfaction; on the other hand, it may be argued (equally plausibly) that absences are a component of overall job satisfaction. Psychologists have occasionally considered absence from a managerial position as behavior to be corrected rather than as the prevalent form of social behavior that it appears to be.

If we search for explanations, we find that few attempts have gone further than a passing reference to social psychological theory. Explanations are offered in isolation from existing theories in social psychology; the results are pseudo theories specific to absence but unrelated to broader theoretical frameworks. This is a situation calling, obviously, for a clear remedy: the placing of absence behavior within its social context, and rejection of the view of absences as an expression of intraindividual motives supposedly available to manipulation.

It follows that an explanation should be derived from theories of social behavior. Hill and Trist's (1962) notion of individual absence behavior as a matter of sequential stages after joining an organization and Vroom's (1964) discussion of choice and absence refer to complex theories of individual behavior. They focus too exclusively on individual motivations. It is true that Hill and Trist recognize a socialization process whereby new employees learn their absence options, how much absence they can safely take. But even this remarkable study is flawed by the use of aggregate (average) statistics in order to expound what is largely a theory of individual motivation. (We shall return to this issue, more extensively, in Chapter 2.)

The fault with many current explanations of absenteeism is that they tend to overemphasize the notion of the individual employee, in the abstract, reacting to work pressures, coping with stress, and facing the organization without benefit of workgroup, peer group, or trade union support (and probably without family or leisure group support). This obviously mythical individual springs from (now rather ancient) management mythology that has an enduring value because it offers a target—the "individual" employee—for manipulation and adjustment strategies, and therefore suits a number of management and consultancy techniques.

_____

*It was estimated that 36 percent were of this kind.

It is also possible to overemphasize the social meaning of absences. For example, Marcuse (1972, p. 21) notes that absenteeism "has reached tremendous proportions"—a sweeping statement that is followed by his interpretation of absenteeism as an expression of rejection by employees of dehumanizing working conditions. Goffman (1968) discusses, as a general phenomenon, the attempt to escape from surveillance, which especially pertains to what he calls "total institutions"—institutions where there is nearly complete surveillance and control over people's activities. People inside these institutions "together lead an enclosed, formally administered round of life"; their location is restricted, their activities are supervised. There may be a few similarities here with the formal supervision and discipline of work environments. Another similarity that may exist between Goffman's "total institutions" and factories or offices is the class cleavage between supervisors and supervised—the former have responsibility and trust, the latter are thought to be irresponsible and unworthy of trust. Goffman points out that the social distance between the two is protected by rules and procedures of the organization: different forms of payment, privileges, and rights.

In institutions that have these conditions of supervision, an escape from surveillance will be much valued: "Where enthusiasm is expected, there will be apathy; where loyalty, there will be disaffection; where attendance, absenteeism; where robustness, some kind of illness; where deeds are to be done, varieties of inactivity" (Goffman 1968, p. 305).

Although this kind of generalization lacks an empirical base, it does seem that absence from work is class-related behavior (see Fox 1976). So far as can be seen from the literature, absenteeism is almost entirely a working-class behavior. It is a question of control over time: the upper and professional classes have relatively unlimited access to time, according to society's rules, whereas hourly paid employees have little control over work time but avail themselves of what they can take, despite the rules.

In general they get around the rules (by taking time off), managing to disregard them to a point where there is a more equitable balance in their trade-off with the organization.

The lower the job status, the sharper the division between work time and personal time. What this means is that there is less flexibility in the ways that hourly paid people can use their time. Costello (1975) makes some rather profound comments relevant to these issues when he suggests that the "right to be absent," to have flexibility in one's working time, is a valued characteristic of professional jobs.

Another point that has plausibility is that a number of consequences follow from lower job status. For instance, people with lower job status are likely to have to wait longer when they seek society's services (Schwartz 1974). Waiting time has to be taken out of leisure periods or taken "illegally" out of working time (because, in any case, many services may not be available non-work hours). Once hourly paid employees have clocked in, they have to stay for the workday;

any other demand on their time—any domestic task, shopping trip, visit to a garage, to a dentist—has, by the rules, to be taken out of off-work time. Those in managerial positions, or in professional and academic positions—and, of course, in the upper classes generally—can take the odd few hours, a half-day, a whole day, to settle these things; they do not need subterfuges or to become "absentees" formally.

"VOLUNTARY" ABSENCES

One very important and primary distinction must be made between voluntary and involuntary absences. (The nature of this distinction, and the rationale for it, will be fully explored in Chapter 4.) It seems sensible to try to distinguish between absences that involve choice and those that do not. The development of discriminating indices of voluntary and involuntary absence constituted one major objective of our research.

A main reason for the interest shown by social scientists in absence from work is that some absences are a direct manifestation of a decision by an employee to withdraw from the work situation. Accidents, turnover, and lateness also are often regarded as related acts of withdrawal, and attention is given in later chapters both to the interrelationship of such indices (Chapter 5) and to theoretical aspects of the notion of withdrawal and to the attempt to achieve precise measures of voluntary absences.

The term "absenteeism," as used in the context of fixed weekly work schedules in factories or offices, usually refers to employee absence that occurs without suitable notification of the employer and without official sanction by medical confirmation of illness. The term itself suggests that much absence from work is voluntary and "avoidable," the result of a decision taken by the employee in disregard of daily work obligations. Absence of this kind may be interpreted as a relief from pressures, or even an aggressive act or a retaliation; it may be an occasional choice of more attractive activities outside of the work place. Always, of course, such choices will be taken within the options made available by the norms and informal standards that have evolved in departments and organizations.

While we have suggested that a category of absences can be termed voluntary, the greatest difficulty occurs in any attempt to find a "pure" measure of voluntary absence (this is discussed in Chapter 4). It soon becomes clear that no measure entirely meets this requirement, although some measures do approach it, as we shall demonstrate. In the arguments based on empirical observations presented as evidence in this book, we advocate the convergent use of several absence measures: summary statistics (summarizing absences for a period of time, Chapters 3 and 5), trend statistics (giving week-by-week profiles, Chapter 3), and correlations (giving a cross-sectional analysis, Chapters 7 and 8).

In Chapter 3 histograms are shown for six absence measures, summarizing absences for different occupations. In Chapters 7 and 8 an intensive correlational study is carried out involving three absence measures: job satisfaction scores and the personal variables of age and length of service. In Chapter 5 five absence measures are intercorrelated and their relationship tested with dispensary attendances. Also examined in Chapter 5 are the statistical (correlational) associations between measures of absence frequency, short-term absences, and "worst day" absences. Given the assumption that they are each, to a large extent, measuring voluntary absences, their close statistical association is demonstrated, thus confirming the assumption.

Throughout the book the basis of absence measurement is always a period of one year, and a variety of absence measures is used consistently. However, the research data are presented in no fewer than four research designs: the summary indices of Chapter 3; the correlational analysis of Chapters 5, 7, and 8; the analysis of trends of Chapter 3, which consist of weekly trends graphed for periods of one calendar year; and interviews with employees in order to reveal their own ideas of explanations about absences (Chapter 3). The exploratory method that is attempted, in Chapter 3, focuses on the reasons that interviewees give for their absences when they talk about them retrospectively to an interviewer. We will be concerned in this analysis with the kinds of reasons that are emphasized, and whether these turn out to be sickness or nonsickness reasons. We will discover that nonsickness absences are purposive, allowing employees to carry out a variety of domestic and leisure activities. In this way we can approach closer to an understanding of the employees' own notions about absences and what kind they consider "normal" for them to take.

The research procedures that we have used—our visits to 80 organizations, the selection of 16 industrial companies and, subsequently, of three banks and two hospitals—are described in Chapter 6 where the treatment of absence records, the administration of questionnaires, the holding of interviews, and the problems of field research are discussed.

We started this research basically to seek evidence for two possible explanations for absenteeism. The first suggested that individual job satisfactions would show an inverse association with absence rates—that is, higher satisfactions would be associated with lower absences and vice versa. This possibility was tested with our correlational analysis. The second suggested that absenteeism could be understood as a group phenomenon, and specifically as part of a social exchange between employees and employers. We explored this possibility in the characteristic absence patterns that we found in different occupations. We sought additional evidence for it in interviews with employees. The approach was exploratory, but it has suggested some practical outcomes. These are discussed in the section "Renegotiating the Norm" of Chapter 9 and in Chapter 10.

2

A THEORY OF ABSENTEEISM

We now present an argument about the meaning and theory of absenteeism that is based on the research evidence we will present below.

Over the past few decades, industrial psychologists have usually presented explanations about individual behavior in terms of looking for the "key" to individual motivation and theorizing about what goes on inside "the worker's" head—seen, incidentally, as a "problem" for managers. Presumably, finding the key could be followed by management's use of it to manipulate worker behavior.

Despite occasional claims of a breakthrough or a general solution, the results of this approach have been disappointing, for the following reasons. Motivations develop within a context of group memberships and affiliations; and the social organization of work, including ideologies of managers and the opposing sentiments of trade union members, can be ignored only by using a relatively superficial analysis. Nevertheless, there has been a good deal of management and "applied psychology" writing suggesting that the correct managerial strategy should consist of providing incentives to individual employees.

Thus, trivialization is the product of management writing that pretends to give managers the key formula. This has been the case for problems, such as absenteeism, where it is fashionable for management consultants to write exhortory papers suggesting incentive plans to reach potential absentees. At one level, that of ideology, this is in itself offensive; on another, a more practical level, it does injury to the concept of absenteeism as a social phenomenon that expresses rules or norms to which individuals collectively refer. In other words, individuals tend to refer to the norm or rule (demonstrations of this will be made in Chapter 3) prescribing how much absence they may have, what forms it can take (one-two days; sickness; nonsickness), and whether it will be accepted by colleagues or tolerated by management.

In this context the absence of one person affects others, and absences are taken only in terms of what is allowed by the occupational "culture." It is true that there may be wide individual differences in frequency and type of absence, but these differences tend to occur inside the limits set by a particular culture. By this use of the word "culture" we mean the beliefs and practices influencing the totality of absences—their frequency and duration—as they currently occur within an employee group or organization (that is, forming a characteristic pattern, as we shall demonstrate in Chapter 3). The nature of this culture is known by employees, though partially and imperfectly, but to that extent absences are regulated by the norm. Thus, the norm is what they collectively recognize (usually with management collusion) as suitable and appropriate for people in their job, their unit, their organization, given the particular conditions, both physical and social, of tasks, pay, status, and discipline.

As we shall argue later, from the evidence we are about to present, absences can be interpreted as part of an exchange among employees as a group and between them and the employing organization. First, among themselves, absences may well be shared out, allocated—"Who else was absent last week?" "Is anyone absent today?" "Is it therefore O.K. for me to be absent tomorrow?" Some forms of alternating behavior may occur here; collusion, no doubt, takes place with supervisors and managers.

Second, between the employees and the employing organization absenteeism is a specific form of exchange, a "negative exchange" unlike the giving of mutual benefits in conventional positive exchanges; here the employees take away, withhold their presence from work. They are very likely, however, to be trading off their absences against work load pressures, boredom, or simply the enormous artificiality—in fact, the enormity—of fixed work schedules.

PREVIOUS THEORIES OF ABSENTEEISM

Gibson (1966) attempted to explain some of the main features of absence behavior by means of the notion of an informal contract. The contract, however, is viewed as being made between individual and organization, and thus largely leaves out the social context of work.

Gibson was especially interested in absences that were not long enough to activate formal legitimizing (certification) procedures. He used the concept of valence, referring to a person's positive or negative relationships to a work situation and pointing out that if the combined valences of a work situation are weak, it will be easier for people to legitimize their absences to themselves. Gibson mentions the plausible idea that the size of an organization influences absence rates: in larger organizations, since there is greater division of labor, there is also more concealment of the contributions of individuals, thus permitting latitude for absence from work. However, a curvilinear relationship was found in some of the data cited by Gibson; this may have been the result of increasing bureaucratic control in the largest organizations. In his discussion Gibson mentions the importance of the employee's identification with the organization, as in the case of longer-service employees, and argues for the importance of the "authenticity" of the work contract—in other words, that the organization should be seen to offer a fair deal to the individual, whose feelings of obligation would thus be strengthened.

However, this notion of "the individual" confronting "the organization" is quite illusory, since individuals will usually be in direct two-person relationships with an employer only in a small business.

Other notable theoretical contributions have been made by Patchen (1960), Adams (1965), and Hill and Trist (1953). The last of these is of great importance, and we shall discuss it in detail.

Adams (1965) suggests that absences may be a means of resolving perceived inequity; the probability of absence behavior will increase with the magnitude of inequity and if other means of reducing inequity are not available. Patchen (1960) had tested this kind of hypothesis, producing evidence of a relationship between absences and perceived fairness of pay (that is, employees' feelings about how fairly they had been treated in regard to their pay levels and promotions).

Hill and Trist (1953; 1962) contributed a theory of absence as withdrawal from the stress of work situations, claiming as evidence for this proposition certain patterns of absence and accident rates recorded over a four-year period in a large steel company. Withdrawal is the central explanatory concept; thus, individuals experiencing conflicts of satisfactions and obligations tend to express them through labor turnover, accidents, and unsanctioned absences (that is, absences without formal permission). Exactly how the conflict will be expressed depends on a sequence of three phases in the employee-organization relationship.

During the early stages of employment, the desire to withdraw is expressed primarily in labor turnover. One important thing, as Hill and Trist point out, in this period is that newcomers are ignorant of the prevalent norms of absences—they do not yet know how far they have this means of withdrawal at their disposal.

After the initial "induction" crisis, the "stayers have had time to learn the prevailing absence culture to the point where they can operate it more freely" (Hill and Trist 1962, p. 34). This is the second phase, which is called "differential transit." Subsequently the relationship stabilizes, as the initial crisis recedes further and the individual reaches a third phase of "settled connection" that has reduced levels of absence.

Thus, the changes in withdrawal behavior are explained by the internalization of norms as individuals become aware of, and party to, the kinds of absence tolerated in the organization. However, if "the available, sanctioned outlets for stress" (absences that the employing authority retrospectively excuses) are insufficient, then hostilities toward the job environment are expressed in accidents and "ailments."

According to Hill and Trist, individuals accept that only so much absence without permission is allowed, and therefore may have recourse to minor illness (which, by the psychoanalytic interpretation, is characteristic of depressive disorder). This is in contrast with the other kind of absence without permission, which reflects a more overt, paranoid expression of hostility. Hill and Trist note that the decline in accident rates with length of service conceals a rise in the numbers of accidents that are under the control of the individual (for example, handling accidents). These represent a depressive mode of feeling and parallel the increase in uncertificated sickness absence as another means of "coping with stress."

Analyzing accident patterns, Hill and Trist account for the relatively low numbers of accidents on night shifts in terms of the reduced degree of authority exercised during that shift.

These explanations are highly speculative, especially because inferences made about individual feelings are not validated in any way. The main fault with the study is that there is a large gap between the level of explanation and the level of the empirical data—in other words, the data consist of collective trends of accidents and absences, while the explanation treats of individual reactions. However, it does constitute an advance in our understanding of absenteeism, notably by the notion that absences are sanctioned by collusive agreements between employers and employees and conform to the normative standards that develop among employees and in organizations.

The "withdrawal" explanation offered by Hill and Trist (1955) had some subsequent influence on theoretical discussions by Knox (1961) and Ås (1962). Gadourek (1965) described the latter as "dynamic conflict" theories. The conflict is located within the individual, and whether a person stays or withdraws is the result of a complex of incentives and stresses. As we have mentioned, the verbal development of the theory by Hill and Trist, in terms of the individual's personality, is "supported" with numerical data at the level of group trends. In other words, the empirical study uses cumulative group data, yet the explanation rests on feelings and conflicts of individuals about which the research study presents no direct information.

To summarize, the main burden of explanation rests on individual conflict and stress, so it appears that the empirical evidence of absence patterns—here the unit of analysis is the group—is to be explained by a theory about "the individual." Thus, the group configuration is held to be the result of intraindividual experience. As a deductive explanation this is acceptable, but still entirely speculative, unless evidence at the individual level is also to be adduced (which in this case has not been done).

It is true that Hill and Trist present individual evidence in the form of each person's absence record, but each record is immediately aggregated with the records of every other person in the group. Once this is done (and only then), they assume a discernible pattern.

Nevertheless, we do not wish to dismiss the Hill and Trist work without further comment. The investigators, despite their use of neo-Freudian interpretations to argue that individual ego defenses against stress are channeled into different forms of withdrawal, do not altogether ignore group explanations.

In fact, they explicitly refer to social norms of absence that, they argue, are internalized by individuals. They also refer to collusion within the organization to produce an "agreed," "normal" level of absenteeism. These are extremely important concepts, and the main fault with Hill and Trist's theoretical discussion is that they have not granted them central importance.

In conclusion, we do not accept the Hill and Trist argument as a general explanation of absenteeism because it tends to reduce explanation to individual internal problems.

Could we now suggest an alternative explanation, at the level of group behavior, without the deductive leap back to individual motivations? In other words, we want an explanation that includes the social context. Given that the empirical material is presented as a group pattern, what, at this level, is the explanation?

We shall now make the case for a theory of absenteeism that is social, not individual, in emphasis. As a first step we assume the interdependency of members of work organizations. This is not a difficult step, because it seems obvious that individuals do have some mutual obligations to peers, subordinates, and superiors (as well as to other relationships outside the work situation). In this context of rights and duties, individuals are both subject to and representative of a set of rules about activities in the work situation. What individuals do is therefore likely to be in answer to, on behalf of, in defense of, and in compromise with these rules of the group. (See Chapter 3 for a discussion of pressures from supervisors, co-workers, or those in the home.)

Our second assumption is that under the employment contract, some form of social exchange is taking place between employers and employees. (For a discussion of social exchange theory, see Chadwick-Jones 1976.) Whatever they exchange in this situation—whether it be their time, effort, or skill for money, security, congenial friends, or anything else—it will be only what is possible for employees in this organization. Exchanges may be conceived as between individuals and work groups, or between work groups and management, but it will not be realistic to conceive of the exchange as between "the individual" and "the organization" while disregarding the social conditions and rules. In summary, then, the group is in the equation—on one or both sides—and the explanation we use must recognize it.

In effect, we have now taken a further theoretical step, this time following the lead of the anthropologists' approach to social exchange, an approach that can be stated succinctly, in the classic terms of Marcel Mauss: "It is groups and not individuals, which carry on exchange, make contracts and are bound by obligations . . . " (1954, p. 3).

We can think of social exchange between employees and employers as developing in, or as revealed by, a pattern of behavior in the work situation that includes absences with all the other factors that constitute the contract, formal and informal, between employers and employees. Formal factors include pay, hours, disciplinary rules, job duties, and promotion lines. Informal ones include supervisory styles, peer group relations, and—salient to our analysis—absences from work. Of course, absences may not enter into the exchange at all, insofar as some employees or employee groups, especially those with higher status—supervisors in factories, managers in banks—are absent very little or hardly at all. It is quite possible, however, that managers possess greater control over the allocation of their working time and may take periods of "time out" that do not get recorded.

Moreover, absences are negative exchange. In the sense that positive exchange involves giving something and receiving something in return, negative exchange requires taking away or withholding something. Thus, absence is understood in relation to the constraints of the work situation. Absence may, for example, be traded against negative factors, such as overly rigid work schedules. (We can infer this from the reasons for absences discussed in Chapter 3.)

In general, then, absences settle at what appear to be collusively acceptable levels, as will be demonstrated in the aggregate analysis of groups presented below.

The advantage of considering absences as part of a social exchange is that this explanation allows for the relatedness of absenteeism to other social factors, whereas an explanation in terms of "individual accommodation" or "individual compensatory behavior" against negative factors tends to isolate the behavior from its social context unless we also recognize that such compensations settle at a level characteristic of the occupational group (see Chapter 3).

Thus far, we have argued that absenteeism levels reflect the social exchange within an organization and that it is "agreed" behavior. This implies that employees understand that their absences should fall within certain limits and, therefore, that their decisions to be absent or to attend conform to a normative frequency level. Employees can be expected to have a definite notion of the appropriate frequency and duration of their absences. The question for them is not only whether to be absent today, but how often they have already been absent this month or this year.

In most cases it can safely be assumed that the act of going absent does not bring with it any punishing consequences, provided it is within the accepted, ongoing pattern of social exchange. In order to deliver deterrent consequences, the organization would require a fine-grained policy of action toward employees that rewards individual attendance while punishing individual absences. Clearly, such contingent and sensitive reactions to absences, on the part of the organization, are seldom likely to be practical. And even if they were, punishments would still be impractical in the face of possible counteraction by employees, in the form of union protest or strikes.

ABSENTEEISM AND SOCIAL EXCHANGE

The application of social exchange theory to absence behavior is appropriate for the following reasons. First, the work contract between employees and employers is, by its nature, a trade-off of gains and costs. Second, evidence that absences are part of this exchange can be adduced from two kinds of research.

On the one hand, we will demonstrate absence distributions suggesting that the majority of employees are conforming to informal "rules" of frequency and duration of absences. This evidence is all the more convincing (as we will see) because it can be shown that such "rules" are distinctive to particular occupations.

On the other hand, we should also collect information about employees' perceptions and understanding of absences that supports the theory. We do not expect employees to say that absences are part of an exchange, but we do expect them to share notions of how much absence is reasonable, to have an idea of whether certain absences are justified and what the justifications are. We mentioned, earlier in the chapter, that in some cases employee feelings about how fairly they have been treated appear to be associated with absences (Patchen 1960). It is clear that such feelings constitute important evidence of a kind that has rarely been presented. In Chapter 3 we will present evidence of patterns of absence behavior and of employees' explanations of it.

In summary, it is intended to show that absences express an element in a social exchange between an employee group and the employing organization. This explanation is supported by the analysis of absence figures and of employees' perceptions of their absences. The exchange explanation could be translated into other, less comprehensive but more specific hypotheses—for example, that "stress produces absence." Plausible ideas of this kind are, in principle, comprehended within the exchange explanation, in that work pressures may well be compensated by increases in absence. But this is a matter for research within an occupational group or organization. We need to establish, first, the aggregate pattern of absenteeism by frequencies, durations, and patterns of incidence in the precise forms that, up to now, we have not had available either on an adequate scale or by adequate measurement.

In our presentation over the following pages we concentrate on demonstrating patterns that support the theory. A statistical analysis demonstrates the existence of absenteeism norms, and probably of collusion between employees and employers in developing "acceptable" absenteeism levels.

In future research we would also need to look closely at whatever substantive criteria of work situations can be described in the form of both social and physical job requirements. In addition, absences are influenced by factors outside the work situation, most obviously by commitments to family or other social activities.

In Chapter 8 we show evidence of the influence of personal characteristics (age, length of service) on the exchange, but this influence can be clearly demonstrated only when these characteristics are shared by sufficient numbers for them to show up in the statistical picture. Thus, gender and age group are obvious characteristics allowing analysis of large categories that will demonstrate clear associations with typical absence patterns. Here the exchange is influenced by commitments to marriage and to children, but differentially between men and women. Previous studies suggest that marriage, with its accompanying responsibilities, is associated with lower absence rates for men and with higher absence rates for women. Hedges (1973) noted that the absence rates of women show life cycle variation, and that the age brackets with highest between-sex differences in absence rates are those that include a large majority of women with children under 18.

In the oldest age groups the frequencies of short-casual absences have been shown to be lower than among the young (see Chapter 8). Differences in absence trends suggest a difference in work expectations between young and old, probably a greater attachment to the work situation in older age brackets, and possibly a weaker commitment by them to social activities of all kinds outside of work.

SOCIAL EXCHANGE VERSUS INDIVIDUAL MOTIVATIONS

Our approach to absenteeism as a social phenomenon rather than an individual one is consistent with the criticisms of overly individualistic theory made by social psychologists.

In the advocacy of our theoretical approach it seems necessary to argue against alternatives and to show through their failings why our approach is to be preferred. One such alternative, a "model" of individual motivations, has been suggested by Steers and Rhodes (1978): their approach is faulty because it overemphasizes the intraindividual determinants of absence.

Steers and Rhodes express the hope that their proposed model will be treated as "a series of propositions suitable for testing" (1978, p. 392). In fact, their use of the term "model" refers mainly to a two-dimensional drawing of short word lists enclosed in rectangular boxes, joined by arrows, the result of which seems to be illustrative only of a wide variety of possibilities.

They suggest that there are two major variables influencing absences: "the employee's motivation to attend" and "the employee's ability to attend." It should by now be clear, from previous reviews of the literature, that any model based on the abstract notion of an "individual employee," irrespective of the industrial and occupational context, is entirely defective. To refer to the employee's "motivation to come to work" as "the primary influence on actual attendance" is at best a banality, and at worst is destructive of a social psychological theory of absence that, as a social phenomenon, it must have.

For Steers and Rhodes the job situation "affecting one's attendance motivation" is a collection of separate elements (for example, job level, job stress, work group size) producing reactions in the form of absences. Unfortunately, their literature review reveals that correlations between these different measures and absences have either been "modest" or "not entirely unanimous" (1978, p. 394).

We do not wish to deny the reality of individual motivations, but to question the usefulness of abstracting them from their social context, because recognizing the individual reality must not be done at the expense of the social reality.

Steers and Rhodes tend to take an abstract view of the individual employee, who appears almost as a passive subject awaiting the delivery of experimental stimuli; there is an excessive emphasis on intraindividual motivations as "affective responses to the job situation" (1978, p. 393). Allied to this is a reductionist delimitation of social behavior to the reactions of isolated individuals; the environment is referred to as a secondary factor "of various internal and external pressures to attend."

If it were a matter of studying skilled job performance, this approach might be the correct one. Conditions for skilled job performance are easily simulated and isolated in the laboratory. But the approach is incorrect when it is a matter of membership in occupational groups and of affiliation to trade unions—when it is a matter of the social implications of absenteeism.

The tendency of organizational psychology to isolate the individual is behaviorist in the (worst) sense of attempting to reduce social phenomena to stimulus-response (S-R) units of reinforcement contingencies, and is not behaviorist in the (best) sense of avoiding impressionistic methods.*

Thus, the essence of the approach is to reduce analysis to small, measurable S-R fragments of behavior suitable for laboratory experiments, but not appropriate for the study of actual social behavior. Perhaps it is unfair to single out Steers and Rhodes for using an overly narrow, atomistic focus, for examples of its extreme effects can be seen in many current writings. Naylor, Pritchard, and Ilgen (1980), who present "a theory of individual behavior within organizations," explicitly use a "stimulus-organism-response" (S-O-R) terminology. This terminology was developed historically (and effectively) in experimental psychology to demonstrate how the organism's functions (measured in response units) are the result of specific independent variables (experimentally created conditions or stimuli). Although it can achieve precise microanalysis of individual unit responses, it has not proved to be suitable for studying social behavior evolving in the interaction of multiple relationships. Although the incentives to borrow S-R or S-O-R terms may be strong because of their scientific respectability, they nevertheless compel a focus on the individual that is too restrictive.

However, in the case of Naylor, Pritchard, and Ilgen, although they ostensibly adopt the surface camouflage of S-O-R terminology, the least convincing feature of their approach is, incongruously, the long conjectural discussion of internal motivations of "the individual." Added to this is the failure of these authors to demonstrate their arguments empirically. Thus, the potentially most valuable aspect of any theoretical discussion—its implications for the collection, ordering, and understanding of research material—is left aside.

---

*Mackenzie (1977), in a critical discussion of behaviorism, recognizes the great achievement of this movement, referring to "the sophisticated contemporary behaviorists" Hebb, Eysenck, Broadbent, and Berlyne with the comment that "the work of these psychologists comprises much of the best of contemporary psychology" (p. 57).

One social element that Steers and Rhodes do take into account is work group size: here the evidence points to more frequent absences in larger work groups. They approximate, in this case, to some hint of how absence might enter into an exchange between employees and their work group or between their work group and the organization. But there is really little evidence available, and what there is, dates mainly from research done in the 1950s.

In Steers and Rhodes's discussion of this and other organizational factors, they continually revert to individual job satisfaction as a key mediating concept—as, for example, when they say that context factors "would be expected to influence absenteeism only to the extent that they altered one's job satisfaction with the job situation" (1978, p. 396). Thus, they miss the possibility of developing a more adequate explanation for absences, despite the mention earlier in their article of the merely tenuous relationship that previous studies had been able to demonstrate between job satisfactions and absence measures. Having pointed to the weak relationships found between job satisfactions and absenteeism, Steers and Rhodes can now only present "attendance motivation" as an alternative explanation, in effect a synonym for "job satisfactions." Although the concept is intended to include external factors (such as constraints and obligations of "extra-mural" activities), no means of assessing these are offered.

Again, in stating that "people come to work with differing values and job expectations," Steers and Rhodes completely miss the all-important socialization effects of entering a new work group or occupation, in which individuals learn what to expect, what to value. The emphasis that Hill and Trist (1962) so perceptively place on socialization into work cultures has been entirely lost, and with it the process by which expectations, formed from prior experience, interact with what is available in the work place.

Steers and Rhodes focus on individual strategies of attendance as these relate to threats of layoff, rewards, or incentives in the job. Conspicuously, in this form of explanation "the individual" is presented as relatively detached from social groups inside and outside work. The authors mention such influences in passing, giving lip service to their existence but making no attempt to consider their strength and forms of operation. In their conclusions Steers and Rhodes return to the facile notion that "highly satisfied employees would probably want strongly to attend, while highly dissatisfied employees would probably want strongly not to attend" (1978, p. 402), which seems to indicate once more the impoverished nature of the model. There have been many studies focusing on job satisfactions and absence measures, seeking the possible correlation of these variables; they have not produced any strong evidence that the approach has been a sound one, and it cannot be denied that they constitute a long record of disappointing results.

For the future, Steers and Rhodes continue with speculations at the intra-individual level: for example, "How important are the various constraints on attendance in moderating the relationship between attendance motivation and actual attendance?" The solutions they offer seem to involve a fragmentary list of variables; each fragment is to be assessed (by methods not specified) for its relative importance: "For example, is an organization's incentive/reward system more influential than the prevailing economic conditions, more than satisfactions?" (1978, p. 402). A more practical approach is suggested by monitoring "the sustained impact of 'behavior modification' on employee attendance" (p. 403), presumably the last hope of an approach that looks at isolated elementary relationships in a stimulus-response fashion.

These exhortations for the future reveal the theoretical poverty of an approach that postulates an employer manipulating rewards and confronting a passive, isolated employee, an ideal subject for behavior modification. Only toward the end do Steers and Rhodes briefly mention "extra-organizational factors (e.g. family responsibilities, pressures and norms; friendship groups; etc)." But at this point little can be saved by throwing them in.

In summary, the intraindividual approach appears to encourage a fragmentary analysis, with as many fragments as there have been variables in the numerous studies in which some form of absence measure (even if unspecified) has been utilized. (See Porter and Steers 1973; Muchinsky 1977.) In its place we must have a theory that gives a clear, attainable objective for research rather than an unlimited list of possibilities.

Thus, within the social exchange framework we have a definite set of areas to be researched that are modest and, therefore, realizable in the practical steps to be followed. First, comparative data on several absence measures can be collected from a range of occupations. Second, the perceptions of employees about absences—that is, employees' own theories of absence—can be analyzed. These are not exhortatory aims, because they are carried out in our research and we discuss them in detail below. Before we do so, there are one or two points to be made about the flaws of current "models" such as the ones we have just discussed.

Intraindividual explanations of absenteeism must fail because absence behavior is interindividual social behavior, as the occupational normative patterns demonstrated below confirm. Thus, a useful theory of absence has to give central importance to group influence patterns and to remove "individual motivation" from the abstract isolation of the intraindividual type of model. Employees' motivations to come to work operate within a context that to a large extent predetermines how much absence the individual will take, how often, and when. Even more important, this context of employee-employer organizational relationships will influence the extent to which absence is available as an option, and certainly the limits to which it is available and the particular forms it will take: sickness, nonsickness, medium-duration, or short-term. This was the point that Hill and Trist (1962) astutely made in their remarkable study.

Another point is raised by Steers and Rhodes's suggestions that more rigorous experimental studies should be carried out. "Experimental" seems to imply, for them, changes introduced into the work situation, whereas careful observation and measurement (without such intervention) could also, in a broader sense, be considered experimental. Given the fact that in job design experiments (for example), most investigators fail "to report both the specific absence measure used and the significance level," Steers and Rhodes's suggestion that such studies be carried out more rigorously seems sensible. But it must also be recognized that the likelihood of psychologists carrying out experimental-interventionist studies within occupational contexts is slight, for the following reason. Researchers have only negligible leverage for gaining access to organizations to the point where they can execute interventionist studies. On the contrary, it is more likely that they will be refused entry or allowed only very limited access to research material (see, for example, the setbacks or restrictions encountered by Scheflen, Lawler, and Hackman 1971; Mikalachki and Chapple 1977; Chadwick-Jones 1981). Realistically, this means researching with such data as can be collected (for example, from personnel records) without requiring organizations to lose employees' working time or to incur additional expenditure for research purposes.

In some industries, probably exceptional cases, quite extensive time periods for research interviews with employees may be approved by the organization without interruption of work schedules (see Chadwick-Jones 1969). However, if this is not allowed—as was the case in the Mikalachki and Chapple (1977) and Chadwick-Jones (1981) research projects—then employees can be interviewed outside working hours (a procedure used for some of the interviews reported on in Chapter 3). Here again, the research design to be followed is essentially a noninterventionist one.

Nevertheless, much interest shown in the topic of absence from work has derived from practical questions of reducing the number of lost working days. Our theoretical discussion also has practical implications. The first has to do with absence control. It is well known that a variety of countermeasures have been tried or recommended to reduce absences (Gaudet 1963), although the successes claimed have always been over the short term. If absenteeism, as we have argued, is understood largely as part of the social behavior of an occupational group, then a reduced level of absence can be obtained only by negotiation with that group and its representatives.

Second, if absences are explained as purposive behavior, produced by and in relation to fixed work schedules, to the extent that this is so, more flexible work schedules may be useful in reducing absences.

We will now consider our research evidence, first for patterns of absenteeism and second for the preferences for absences of different kinds. Later in the book, we will again take up the questions concerning absence control involving renegotiation and flexible hours.

3

AN ETHOLOGY OF ABSENTEEISM

In this chapter we present the summarized and grouped absence records of 6,411 employees in six industries, four British (foundries, clothing manufacture, automated process, and public transport) and two Canadian (banks and hospitals).

First, we summarize six measures of absence for a period of one year (total days lost; short term, one to two days; total frequency, irrespective of duration; short-term as a proportion of total frequency; average length of absences; percentages of employees with no short-term absences). By applying these measures we can demonstrate a clear and precise profile of absenteeism in each occupational group, summarized for the period of one year. This will be done in Figures 3.1–3.6, in which we are able to identify normative and distinctive patterns for each occupational group.

Second, in Figures 3.7–3.17 we show the absence trends for three measures, week by week, over one year. These measures are total days lost, short-term (one- or two-day) absences, and absence frequency, irrespective of duration. The weekly trends again show distinctive occupational patterns.

These data are consistent with the inference that absences are part of an informal contract, a trade-off between employee groups and the employing organization, given the existing working conditions (arduous physical conditions in foundries, good health conditions in banks, and so on). The prevailing patterns of absences (how long, how many, and when), it can be assumed, have evolved in a particular working situation and set of job demands, and the absence "options" available are discovered by new entrants to each occupation. As Hill and Trist (1962) suggested, newcomers probably learn how many absences, of what duration, are at their disposal—the length and number of absences that are treated as "normal" within their organization. This form of collusion leads, in banks and hospitals, to widely distributed and frequent short absences, whereas in some blue-collar industries the norm exists for relatively infrequent short absences but a greater number of longer ones.

Figures 3.1-3.6 give ranges of absence indices, from smallest to largest, by industry. These are grouped so that the lowest organization indices are presented for each of the six occupational groups. Thus, for clothing manufacture, foundries, automated process, and public transport the highest and lowest indices are given for the four organizations in each of these industries (16 organizations in all). For banking the highest and lowest indices are given for the three organizations that were sampled; for hospitals, the indices represent one large general hospital and a smaller, highly specialized pediatric hospital. The numbers 991 (clothing), 1,215 (foundries), 1,372 (automated process), 1,226 (public transport), 666 (banking), and 941 (hospitals), making a total of 6,411 employees, in 21 organizations, whose absence records were analyzed for a period of one year.

Figure 3.1 gives the Time-Lost Index. This is a standard measure presenting the total number of days lost per 100 people per 100 weeks. Highest sickness rates in foundries and public transport result in these industries having the highest indices. As might be expected with excellent physical working conditions

FIGURE 3.1

**Total Time Lost Index:
Highest and Lowest Indices Within the Industry**

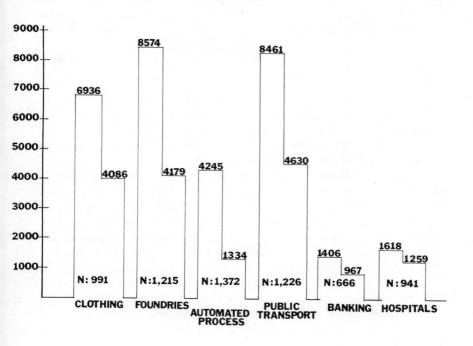

FIGURE 3.2

Frequency Index:
Highest and Lowest Indices Within the Industry

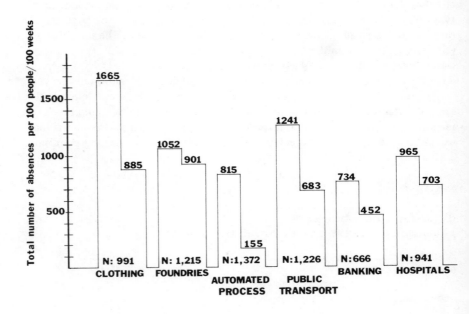

and a younger employee population, banks have the lowest index. Hospitals show a similar tendency to relatively low sickness levels.

Figure 3.2 gives the Frequency Index, computed for the total number of absences per 100 people per 100 weeks.

Women employees in clothing manufacture have the highest absence frequencies, and public transport (males) are second highest. The lowest frequency was in one of the automated process (oil) companies. Banks here fall in the lower-middle range. It should be noted that employees in clothing manufacture, banks, and hospitals were, in the great majority, females: 77 percent in banks (513 of a total of 666); in hospitals there were 94 percent females (887 of a total of 941); the entire work force samples in clothing manufacture were female.

Figure 3.3, the Short-Term Index shows the total number of one- and two-day absences, computed in standard fashion. Clothing manufacture has by far the highest figure on this index, and automated process the lowest, with the other industries appearing in middle ranges. Of the latter, public transport and hospitals have the highest indices.

It is not until we examine Figure 3.4, the "Cleans" Index, that we discover the distinctive pattern of absences in banks and hospitals. The "Cleans" Index is the percentage of employees not having any one- or two-day absences during a year. In banks and hospitals, short absences are very widely distributed. In one bank 10 percent of its employees did not have any short absences during the year, a proportion similar in size to some firms in clothing manufacture. Furthermore, the pediatric hospital had only 11 percent of absence-free employees (out of a total of 218 nurses and 104 administration staff); in the large general hospital only 6 percent of 619 employees (554 nurses, 65 ancillary grades, mainly ward clerks) had no short-term absences. (The distributions for the general hospital and one of the banks are shown in detail in Figures 9.1 and 9.2.)

On the other hand, in one public transport company about half the employees had no short-term absences, and in one organization in automated industry no less than 75 percent of all employees had no short absences.

It is notable that the occupations with lowest proportions of absence-free

FIGURE 3.3

Short-Term Index:
Highest and Lowest Indices Within the Industry

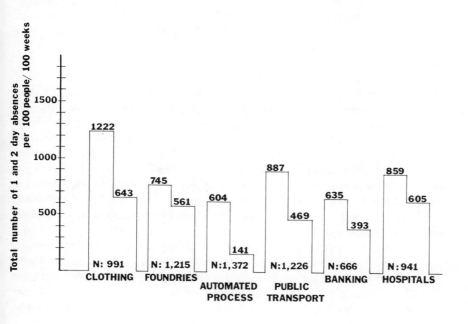

FIGURE 3.4

"Cleans" Index:
Highest and Lowest Indices Within the Industry

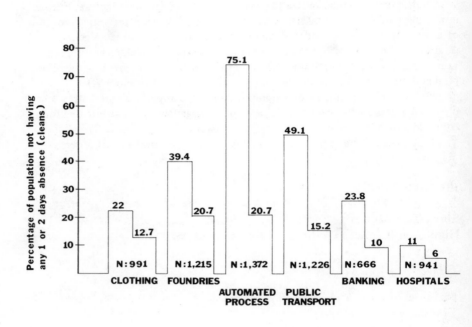

employees are those with mainly female workers. This conforms to conclusions drawn in Chapters 2 and 9 concerning the greater share of responsibility allocated to women for family and domestic maintenance tasks.

Figure 3.5, which shows the mean length of absence, supports the indications revealed by Figure 3.4: the mean lengths of absences in banks and hospitals are much shorter than in any of the other industries, one bank having 1.7 days as its average and both hospitals having similar lengths of absence. At the other extreme, an automated process plant shows an average of just over 14 days per absence.

Thus, a "white-collar" pattern emerges as one of extremely widespread, very short, nonsickness absences.

Figure 3.6, which concerns the number of one- and two-day absences as a percentage of total frequency, corroborates the picture of widespread, occasional, short absences among white-collar employees. In the banks short-term absences constitute between 87 and 91 percent of all absences; in hospitals the proportions are between 86 and 89 percent, substantially above the percentages presented for any of the blue-collar occupations.

FIGURE 3.5

Mean Length of Absence:
Highest and Lowest Indices Within the Industry

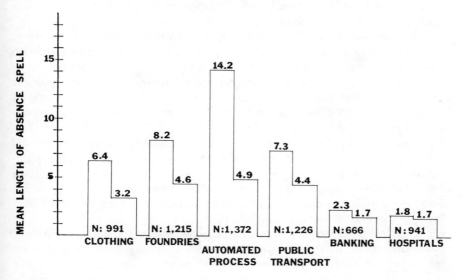

FIGURE 3.6

Number of One- and Two-Day Absences as Percentage of Total
Frequency: Highest and Lowest Indices Within the Industry

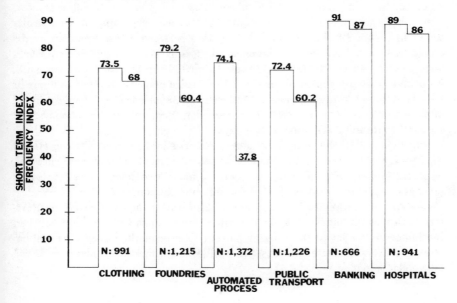

WEEK-BY-WEEK TRENDS

In addition to the summaries of six different yearly absence indicators that we have just discussed, the week-by-week trends in absences clearly demonstrate the same characteristic occupational patterns.

In Figures 3.7–3.17 the unbroken line represents total days lost per week; the broken lines represent absences starting in that week (frequency), and also one- or two-day absences (short-term).

Particularly noticeable are the higher levels of longer-term sickness absences in some blue-collar industries. For instance, in Figure 3.7 the weekly graph for January–December shows the total days lost (time lost) line well above frequency totals and short-term absences.

This contrasts with the banks and hospitals (largely female occupational groups), and to some extent with the absence profiles among clothing manufacture (assembly-line) female employees (in two out of the four organizations studied in that industry). However, the contrast is not so marked for the latter, since in the other two clothing organizations longer sickness absences are moderately frequent (as we will illustrate below).

Figures 3.8–3.10 exhibit characteristic trend patterns for employees in three banks over one year. The characteristic pattern is repeated in the trend analyses we carried out within all three banks for a number of their local branches. The trend is always for longer-term absences, the time-lost index (TLI), to be relatively lower than short (one- or two-day) absences and lower than the frequency totals, which are, in the bank trends, made up largely of short absences. The trends are almost identical in each of the three banking organizations.

To give some idea of what these weekly indices mean in terms of actual absentees, we can examine the frequency rates of Figure 3.8. It will be recalled that the frequency measure represents all absences beginning in a particular week. In Figure 3.8 the frequencies show that between 7 and 8 percent of the employees started a period of absence during the weeks in which frequencies were at their highest: In January (week 3), out of 386 employees in this bank, 32 people started a period of absence; 27 of them stayed away for only one or two days. In week 7, 29 people started an absence period, 28 of them returning after one or two days. In week 47 (November), 28 people started absences and 25 of them returned after one or two days.

In Figure 3.10 the frequency rates, at their highest, varied between 10 and 12.5 percent. For example, in week 2, six people started their absences; in week 5, seven; in week 13, eight; and in week 36, nine. In all these cases employees (except one in week 36) were absent for only one or two days.

In the two hospitals the frequency totals (again composed largely of short-term absences) are higher than in the banks, although the relationship between the indices is similar to the banking pattern. The graphs for these two occupations present a characteristic absence profile and a marked contrast with the blue-collar trends.

FIGURE 3.7

Weekly Absence Trends in an Automated Plant

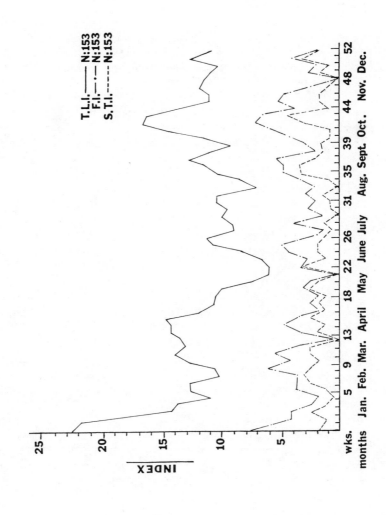

FIGURE 3.8

Weekly Absence Trends in a Bank

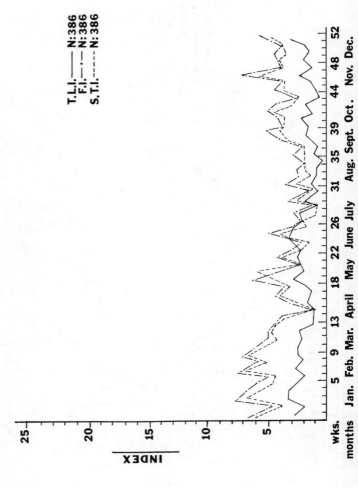

T.L.I. —— N:386
F.I. —·— N:386
S.T.I. ----- N:386

INDEX

25
20
15
10
5

wks. 5   9 13 18 22 26 31 35 39 44 48 52
months Jan. Feb. Mar. April May June July Aug. Sept. Oct. Nov. Dec.

FIGURE 3.9

Weekly Absence Trends in a Bank

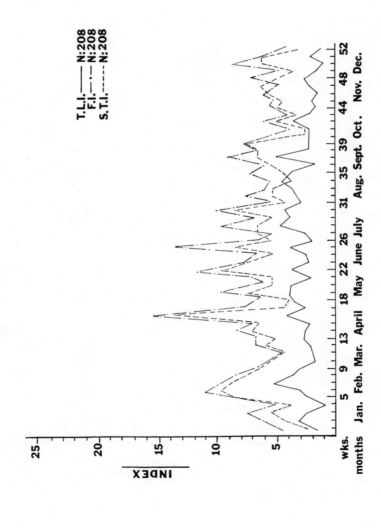

27

FIGURE 3.10

Weekly Absence Trends in a Bank

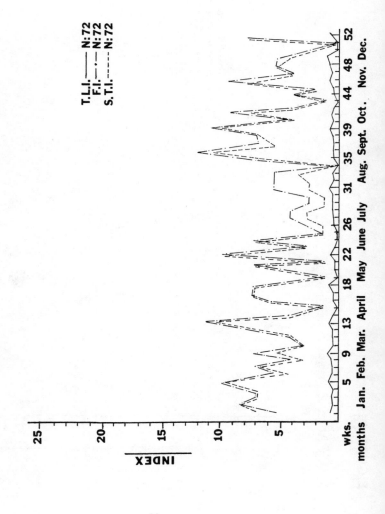

FIGURE 3.11

Weekly Absence Trends Among Nurses

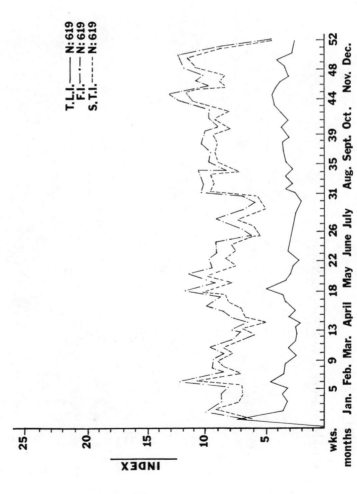

29

FIGURE 3.12

Weekly Absence Trends Among Nurses

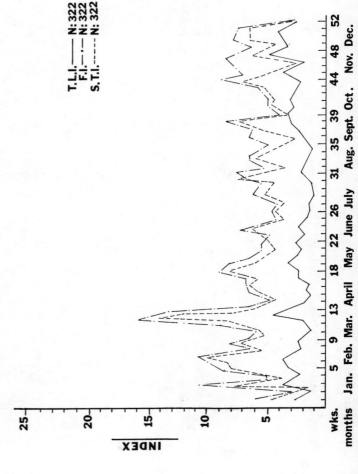

FIGURE 3.13

Weekly Absence Trends in Clothing Manufacture

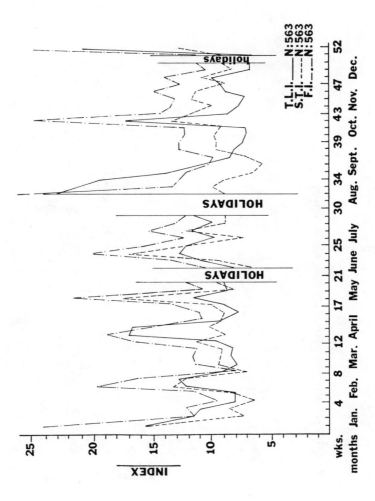

FIGURE 3.14

Weekly Absence Trends in Clothing Manufacture

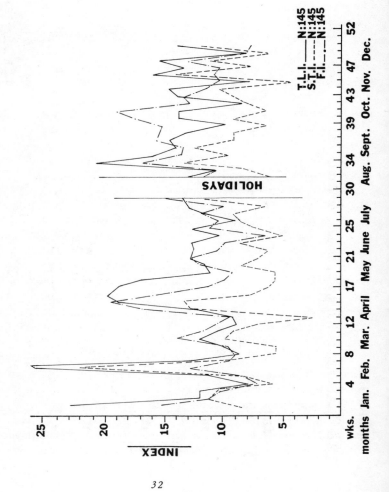

32

As was mentioned above, women employees in two clothing manufacturing organizations showed a similar relative relationship of the indices (higher short-term absences), as Figure 3.13 illustrates. However, the pattern is not such a clear one, because longer-term absences are high at some points. Figure 3.14 shows a heavy record of absences of all kinds for clothing manufacture.

SEASONAL AND SYSTEMATIC FLUCTUATIONS

Each of the figures reveals seasonal fluctuations—for example, a heavier incidence of absences during some of the winter months. More important, however, systematic patterns are discernible. For example, in our analysis of the absences of employees in clothing manufacture, both frequency and short-term absences were found to coincide with school holidays and with husbands' holidays during July. Many women took a short holiday a week or two before the official spring (Easter) break, and there were sharp rises before and after the Christmas holiday period.

These systematic fluctuations showing the importance, in absenteeism, of commitments to home and family also illustrate (and this is more important to our argument) the purposive nature of absence from work. Thus, they tend to substantiate the view that many absences involve deliberate decisions to take time off.

Our main conclusion from the presentation of these graphs must be that there are characteristic differences in the occupational patterns. The most remarkable of the results is the clear indication of a banking pattern, a hospital pattern, a clothing manufacturing (or assembly line) pattern, and so on, as well as the overall white-collar and blue-collar differences.

The distinctiveness of the bank employees' and the nurses' patterns is demonstrated further when these are compared with an equally characteristic but reverse pattern in blue-collar industries. For example, in Figure 3.15, employees of an oil company show relatively more long-term sickness but lower frequency totals and fewer short-term absences. Figure 3.16 presents this same tendency for a small public transport company. In Figure 3.17 the graph for a foundry reveals longer duration rates, with the frequency and short-term indices running far lower. A similar pattern is shown for employees of a large public transport firm in Figure 3.18. (Figures 3.15–3.18 are included to illustrate consistent patterns in the blue-collar groups and to underline the contrast with the banks and hospitals.)

This evidence is consistent with a "trade-off" or exchange interpretation of absenteeism, with consensus among employees and collusion between employees and employers concerning the appropriate levels of absences, in a given context of job requirements and working conditions. What it does not do, of course, is provide direct evidence. It does not "prove" the case. It does give an indirect and reasonably convincing indication that absenteeism is group-influenced behavior. However, the group influences include social-physical conditions of work—envi-

FIGURE 3.15

Weekly Absence Trends in an Automated Plant

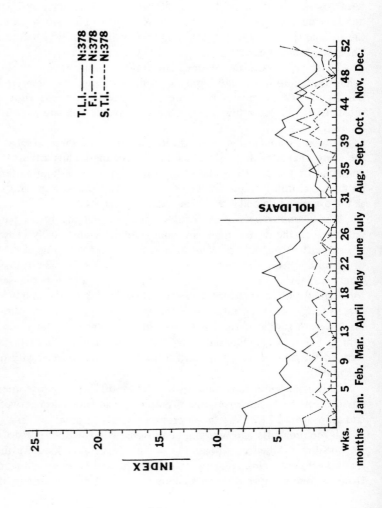

FIGURE 3.16

Weekly Absence Trends in a Public Transport Organization

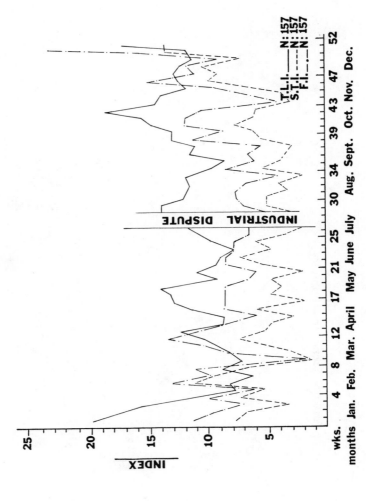

FIGURE 3.17

Weekly Absence Trends in a Foundry

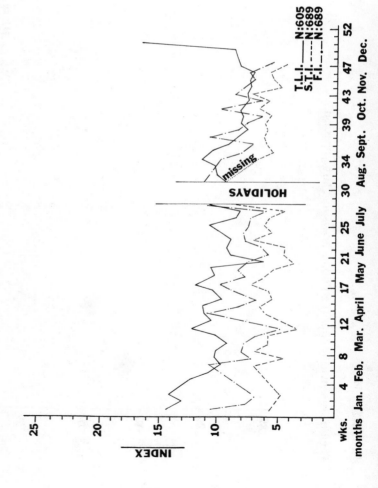

FIGURE 3.18

Weekly Absence Trends in a Public Transport Organization

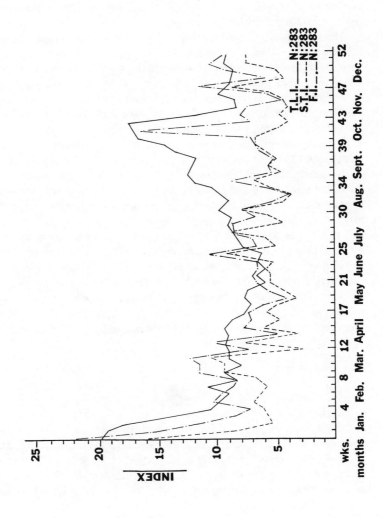

ronmental factors, the extent to which the work itself is physically or mentally demanding. In other words, the working conditions shared by employees are influential in producing a given pattern of brief, casual, or longer-term sickness absences.

Thus, patterns emerge when we focus attention on the group aggregate statistics. At this level individual choices appear to conform to some notion of a rule, among employees, concerning what kinds or frequencies of absences are appropriate in their work situation. It would clearly be useful in the future to focus attention on the operation of individual variations within the limits set by the social-physical context of the occupational group. Data that have been presented earlier in this chapter (and are presented in Chapter 9)—such as the proportions of absence-free employees and the distribution of absences within an occupational group—are important indicators of the social constraints and options within particular occupations.

In conclusion, the evidence presented suggests an interpretation of absence behavior as a social phenomenon and seems to indicate some degree of conformity to "rules" that govern how much absence, duration of absence, and on which occasions absences are both appropriate (from the employees' point of view) and acceptable (to management) within a given organization and occupation.

The distinctive patterns of absence have been shown in several occupational contexts. In the trend analysis we found, in the case of young mothers, a pattern of absences during and around school holidays, elections (when schools are closed), and the periods of husbands' holidays. Occasions such as these are relatively banal, but they give us an explanation of a proportion of absence frequencies when there are peaks in the pattern. Incidentally, absences that allow people to meet their domestic responsibilities are further evidence that absenteeism is purposive, as is also suggested by the interviews.

It remains to explore the evidence gathered from interviews with employees by analyzing the reasons that interviewees give for their absences when they talk about them retrospectively to a researcher. We are interested in the kinds of reasons that are emphasized, and whether these are sickness or nonsickness reasons. It may also be that we can arrive at some understanding of employees' own notions of what kinds of absences they consider "normal." At the moment, in the absence literature generally, there seems to be a dearth of such information.

INTERVIEWS

We conducted 488 interviews with direct production workers in the blue-collar (British) organizations and 231 interviews with white-collar workers and nurses in Canada. In clothing manufacturing whole lines of women machine operators were selected whose work was typical of the plant. They included approximately equal proportions of young, single and older, married women. In the foundries interviewees were usually molders and fettlers (metal dressers), and in the automated plants they were the higher grade operators. In public transport companies representative proportions of drivers, conductors, and one-man operators were selected at random. As is described in Chapter 6, the management in banks refused permission for interviews, and it was not thought advisable to request interviews in the hospitals. Canadian interviewees consisted of 151 office workers in a variety of organizations, interviewed at random outside their work situations by a team of student researchers who also interviewed 40 nurses and 40 bank employees under similar conditions.

Interviewees were asked general questions about absences from work, both their own and those of their colleagues. These questions were intended to be exploratory, in that the replies would show us what employees thought about occasional absences and the most likely reasons for occasional days off from work. We were interested in the latter because of the insights these interviews might give us into the meaning of absenteeism—the reality of it—for the absentees themselves. This technique would not prove anything; we assumed it would suggest useful avenues for future research. But the picture it revealed turned out to be consistent with, and even explicitly supportive of, the social exchange explanation of absenteeism.

In our discussion below we have divided the reasons given for absences into two categories of purposive reasons (domestic responsibilities, business errands) and personal, episodic ones (minor illness, boredom, or pressure). We are no nearer, in our discussion of this tentative and exploratory evidence, to linking reasons with absence rates. But we are able to show some consistent indicators of the meaning of absenteeism as seen by employees.

The purposive reasons—coping with home maintenance or children's needs, keeping business or shopping appointments—easily constitute around half of all the reasons given for being absent, both in the blue-collar (British) samples and in the white-collar (Canadian) samples. Table 3.1 gives the distribution of reasons in the four blue-collar industries.

It should be noted that Table 3.1 reveals a high prevalence of domestic reasons, after illness, for absences among all groups, not just the female workers in clothing manufacture. In fact, the highest percentage of domestic reasons was found in public transport. Whatever the reason, this group is more available for domestic responsibilities; these results suggest that the importance of domestic pressures may have been underrated by previous researchers. Clearly, the question of family crisis management is one that should be explored; this kind of research has scarcely been attempted.

The replies to the question "For what reasons would you take a day off work?" were placed in seven categories, according to their content and by number of respondents mentioning each topic. Most could be grouped under "Illness," "Domestic reasons," "Business," and personal or episodic feelings—feeling bored, feeling tired, wanting a break. The residual category "Other reasons" consisted of miscellaneous reasons such as attending football games and going on shopping expeditions. The descriptions used for coding the replies into each category are as follows:

TABLE 3.1

Blue-Collar Self-Reports: Reasons for Absences
(N = 488)

	Clothing (N = 165)		Foundries (N = 62)		Automated (N = 120)		Public Transport (N = 141)	
	No.	Percent	No.	Percent	No.	Percent	No.	Percent
Illness	84	50.9	30	48.4	68	56.7	69	48.9
Domestic reasons	53	38.2	16	25.8	43	35.8	64	45.4
Business	23	13.9	8	12.9	6	5.0	20	14.2
Feeling tired	15	9.1	9	14.5	6	5.0	28	19.9
Feeling bored	54	32.7	6	9.7	12	10.0	10	7.1
Wanting a break	13	7.9	7	11.3	9	7.5	17	12.1
Other reasons	25	15.2	10	16.1	18	15.0	28	19.9

Interview question: "For what reasons would you take a day off work?"
Chi square = 59.12; d.f. = 18; $p < .001$.

Illness—any response indicating the only major cause of absence to be the respondent's own incapacity for work resulting from some identifiable ailment

Domestic reasons—events and situations at home that prompt absence, such as illness in the family

Business—absences taken to enable the respondent to attend to some business that could not be handled easily outside work time, from house purchase or legal matters to dental appointments

Feeling bored—any indication that absence is taken to avoid some negatively evaluated aspect of work

Feeling tired—instances of absence to relieve the cumulative fatigue of work attendance—that is, absence as a form of relief or "refreshment"

Wanting a break—genuinely "casual" absence where the respondent "just felt like a day off"

Other reasons—these comprise miscellaneous reasons for absence—for instance, in order to attend a football game or go on a shopping expedition.

In Tables 3.2-3.4 we show the distribution of "reasons for absence" perceived by office workers, bank employees, and nurses. We gave respondents a checklist of 14 items and asked them to indicate which were their usual reasons for absence. Reasons were as follows: serious domestic problems, boring job, date with friends, feeling depressed, minor domestic problems, disagreement with co-workers, minor ailments, community activities, sports, accidents, business, disagreement with boss, job pressures, waking up late.

Table 3.2 shows reasons given most often by office workers from a variety of organizations, and Table 3.3 gives a similar breakdown for bank employees. Table 3.4 presents the reasons given most often by nurses.

The distributions in all three samples are very similar. Accidents are mentioned most frequently by office workers and bank employees, but domestic problems would be preponderant if we were to group serious and minor problems together. The total effect of these reasons for taking time off, in both the blue-collar and the white-collar groups, is to suggest that much absence is the result of purposive (domestic problems, business) and episodic (relief from pressure, boredom) choices.

Purposive choices (allowing time for responsibilities, activities) are by far the majority. However, episodic choices are always present, and they show the importance of absences in providing relief from boredom and depression. These personal reasons occurred least often in the automated plants and most often in the repetitive jobs of clothing manufacture. Among bank employees as well as office workers, the references to depression seem to convey a situation where individuals are trapped in limited, uninteresting jobs. This feeling is expressed by one-third of the office workers (51), 22 males and 29 females. Very few people express outright dislike for their jobs, as shown in Table 3.5.

TABLE 3.2

Office Workers' Perceived Reasons for Absences (N = 151)

	Total	Percent	No. Mentioning			
			Male	Percent	Female	Percent
Accidents	111	73.50	50	76.92	61	70.93
Serious domestic problems	109	72.18	43	66.15	66	76.74
Minor ailments	95	62.91	46	70.76	49	56.97
Business	76	50.33	36	55.38	40	46.51
Feeling depressed	51	33.77	22	33.84	29	33.72
Job pressures	43	28.47	18	27.69	25	29.06
Boring job	37	24.50	20	30.76	17	19.76
Minor domestic problems	25	16.55	13	20.00	12	13.95
Waking up late	23	15.23	12	18.46	11	12.79
Community activities	20	13.24	15	23.07	5	5.81
Sports	17	11.25	13	20.00	4	4.65
Disagreement with co-workers	12	7.94	3	4.61	9	10.46
Date with friends	10	6.62	6	9.23	4	4.65
Disagreement with boss	7	4.63	2	3.07	5	5.81

Interview question: "Why do people usually have to take time off?"
Sample consists of 86 females, 65 males.
Mean age: males, 36.77 years; females, 30.2 years.
Mean length of service: 9 years.

TABLE 3.3

Bank Employees' Perceived Reasons for Absences
(N = 40)

	No. Mentioning	Percent
Accidents	34	85
Minor ailments	31	77.5
Serious domestic problems	29	72.5
Business	19	47.5
Job pressures	11	27.5
Minor domestic problems	9	22.5
Boring job	8	20
Feeling depressed	8	20
Waking up late	6	15
Sports	3	7.5
Community activities	3	7.5
Disagreement with boss	2	5
Disagreement with co-workers	1	2.5
Date with friends	1	2.5

Interview question: "Why do people usually have to take time off?"
Sample consists of 31 females and 9 males.
Mean age: 31.5 years.
Mean length of service: 8 years.

Frequently, references were made in interviews to the calculating aspect of absence decisions. For example, a 26-year-old female employee of an insurance company, discussing management policy toward absences with pay, stated:

A person thinks twice about how badly they need time off when you must lose a day's pay. So the most time a person takes off a month is one day, unless absolutely necessary. However, in many cases a person will take two days off at a time, since they lose one day's pay anyway. Perhaps they feel it's a way to make up for the loss.

A 21-year old secretary put the matter more explicitly:

Management try to control absences. With our own contract we can only be ill on three separate occasions. If we are ill on a fourth or a fifth time we lose the first day's pay. The result often works the other way, though—if we are ill the fourth time and miss one day, knowing we won't be paid, we might as well stay off another day because we are paid for all but the first day.

TABLE 3.4

Nurses' Perceived Reasons for Absences
(N = 40)

	No. Mentioning	Percent
Serious domestic problems	34	85
Accidents	33	82.5
Minor ailments	30	75
Job pressures	26	65
Business	17	42.5
Feeling depressed	13	32.5
Waking up late	11	27.5
Minor domestic problems	10	25
Boring job	6	15
Date with friends	5	12.5
Sports	3	7.5
Disagreement with boss	2	2.5

Interview question: "Why do people usually have to take time off?"
Sample consists of 39 females, 1 male.
Mean age: 36.5 years.
Mean length of service: 8 years.

TABLE 3.5

Degree of Liking Expressed for Job by Office Workers
(N = 151)

	Total	Percent	Male		Female	
			No.	Percent	No.	Percent
Like it very much	46	30.46	23	37.70	23	28.05
Like it	68	45.03	26	42.62	42	51.22
Neither like it nor dislike it	25	16.56	9	14.76	16	19.51
Dislike it	3	1.99	2	3.28	1	1.22
Dislike it very much	1	0.66	1	1.64		
Not ascertained	8	5.30				

Interview question: "In general, how do you feel about your job?"

A 50-year-old male employee of the federal government came near to an explicit mention of a retaliatory exchange between employees and managers:

> It varies depending on the supervisor and type of work . . . a hard-nosed approach causes resistance and a sense of getting revenge ("I'll just take a day off for that!")

A 54-year-old female employee of the federal government felt that

> They go along, everything is tolerated, measures are not taken to rectify situations. It does not vary from office to office, it's a general disease.

Many white-collar workers felt that management was mainly tolerant of absences. As one pointed out, "In my office it is not that important; also, they—the management—take their own days off."

Are absences justified? Interviewees were asked their feelings about whether occasional absences were or were not justified. Among the office workers (N = 151) serious domestic problems, accidents, minor ailments, and business reasons were all mentioned by 50 or more employees as causes of justified absences. The most frequently mentioned unjustified causes were feeling bored or depressed (134), waking up late (104), disagreement with co-workers (70), and disagreement with boss (66).

Blue-collar workers were asked a question about the legitimacy of "taking a day off when you feel like a break from the routine of work." Did they consider this occasional day justified or unjustified? We see the results of this question in Table 3.6, where the answers are tabulated according to whether employees judged such absences to be "justified" or "unjustified."

In the automated plants, where short, occasional absences were fewest, this kind of absence was viewed with greatest disapproval. Public transport employees appeared to judge one-day absences less favorably than did workers in clothing manufacturing or foundries, where large majorities definitely considered them to be justified.

It was possible that management policy in granting permission for absences—and whether it was obtained easily or with difficulty—might have influenced general absence levels. In foundries, automated plants, and public transport, employees were therefore asked whether permission for absence was easy or difficult to obtain. Table 3.7 shows foundries as having the most "facilitating" managerial policy in this respect. In public transport the large number of other replies included many people who said they did not know how easy it was to obtain permission, some commenting in terms like "I never bother to ask, in case it is refused. I just take one."

Employees in foundries and automated plants were asked whether absences affected supervisors (Table 3.8). The foundry replies (52 percent "absence affects supervisors," as against 39 percent in automated process) suggested more marked

TABLE 3.6

Blue-Collar Employees' Perceptions of Occasional One-Day Absences

	Clothing (N = 165)		Foundries (N = 62)		Automated (N = 120)		Public Transport (N = 141)	
	No.	Percent	No.	Percent	No.	Percent	No.	Percent
"Justified"	113	68.48	47	75.81	41	34.16	73	51.77
"Unjustified"	48	29.09	15	24.19	71	59.17	62	43.97
Other replies	4	2.43	0	0.0	8	6.67	6	4.26

Chi square = 44.13; d.f. = 3; p < .001.

TABLE 3.7

Perceived Ease of Permission for Absence: Blue-Collar Jobs

	Foundries (N = 62)		Automated (N = 120)		Public Transport (N = 141)	
	No.	Percent	No.	Percent	No.	Percent
Permission easily obtained	51	82.26	73	60.83	63	44.68
Permission difficult to obtain	4	6.45	36	30.00	34	24.11
Other replies	7	11.29	11	9.17	44	31.21

Interview Question: "Is it easy or difficult to get time off?"
Chi square $= 40.20$; d.f. $= 4$; $p < .001$.

effects on supervisors. And, as might be expected in the more sophisticated technologies, first-line supervisors figure rather less in automated production.

A further question was asked about whether supervisors commented on absences (Table 3.9). In public transport only 32 percent of employees said that supervisors would make any comment on their absences; this could be taken as possible evidence of management collusion among the remainder. A larger minority in foundries (40 percent) felt that supervisors would comment on absences, while in automated plants 48 percent reported comments of some kind.

Last, the workers in automated plants and public transport personnel were asked whether they would try to comply with supervisory pressures to be at work (Table 3.10). In public transport only 7 percent admitted to paying any attention to supervisors' pressures, and in automated process 22 percent reported

TABLE 3.8

Perceived Effects of Absence on Supervisors

	Foundries (N = 62)		Automated (N = 96)	
	No.	Percent	No.	Percent
Absence affects supervisor	32	51.61	37	38.54
Other replies	30	48.39	59	61.46

Chi square n.s.

TABLE 3.9

Workers Reporting That Supervisors Comment on Their Absence

	Foundries (N = 62)		Automated (N = 96)		Public Transport (N = 138)	
	No.	Percent	No.	Percent	No.	Percent
Supervisors comment on absence	25	40.32	46	47.92	44	31.88
Other replies	37	59.68	50	52.08	94	68.12

Chi square = 6.65; d.f. = 2; p < .05.

doing so. These percentages complete the picture of little or no supervisory intervention in this area of employee behavior.

Even fellow workers in foundries and public transport reacted very little to absences. Employees asked if their co-workers would comment on their absence (Table 3.11) reported in the affirmative only to the extent of 18 percent in foundries and 15 percent in public transport. In automated plants 42 percent said co-workers would do so, this latter result confirming our information received from other sources on the interdependence of work teams in the advanced technology organizations, such as oil and plastics.

TABLE 3.10

Reported Compliance with Pressure to Be at Work from Supervisors

	Automated (N = 64)		Public Transport (N = 141)	
	No.	Percent	No.	Percent
Try to comply with pressure to attend	14	21.88	1	7.09
Other replies	50	78.12	131	92.91

Chi square = 11.36; d.f. = 1; p < .001.

TABLE 3.11

Workers Reporting That Co-workers Comment on Their Absence

	Foundries (N = 62)		Automated (N = 120)		Public Transport (N = 123)	
	No.	Percent	No.	Percent	No.	Percent
Co-workers comment on absence	11	17.74	50	41.67	18	14.63
Other replies	51	82.26	70	58.33	105	85.37

Chi square = 26.06; d.f. = 2; p < .001.

INFLUENCES OUTSIDE THE WORK SITUATION

Questions in the interviews were aimed at revealing the influence of encouragement from home (from spouse or parents) to go to work or to stay at home "when in two minds about whether to go into work." Table 3.12 reveals, principally, a marked difference in the pressures on female and male workers.

About half of each group says that the decision to go to work or not is left to them (other replies); only in the (female) clothing manufacturing group is there substantial encouragement to stay at home. In all the male occupations the predominant pressure is toward going to work, most strongly in the case of the automated process workers.

Although, as we saw in Table 3.1, domestic reasons for absences are not reported more frequently by women in the blue-collar samples, this does appear to be the case for the office workers (Table 3.2), where 44 percent of females mention serious domestic problems (as against 29 percent of males). But in Table 3.12 the replies certainly suggest that pressures from home are clearly on the side of womens' greater share of domestic responsibilities. This is consistent with the higher frequencies (shown earlier in this chapter) of short-term absences in clothing manufacture, banks, and hospitals, where most employees are female.

CONCLUSIONS

Accidents outside of work were frequently given as one major (if conventional) reason for absence, as was sickness, but most of the reasons that our interviewees gave were purposive: time to see to business and domestic matters, greater access to leisure. There was, relatively, a smaller proportion of episodic reasons in each sample—for example, feeling depressed or bored. Here absences were a relief from the pressure of fixed hourly schedules.

TABLE 3.12

Direction of Reported Pressures When "in Two Minds" About Work Attendance

	Clothing (N = 165)		Foundries (N = 62)		Automated (N = 120)		Public Transport (N = 141)	
	No.	Percent	No.	Percent	No.	Percent	No.	Percent
Encouraged to stay at home	68	41.21	10	16.13	19	15.83	24	17.02
Encouraged to go to work	20	12.12	18	29.03	42	35.00	38	26.95
Other replies	77	46.67	34	54.84	59	49.17	79	56.03

Chi square = 40.20; d.f. = 4; p < .001.

We have presented and discussed two kinds of evidence, analytical (histograms, trend analysis) and exploratory (interviews). In the empirical results, absences, whether purposive or episodic, have been shown to converge into group patterns. Both kinds of evidence were entirely consistent with our argument that absences are often part of a social exchange.

4

THE CONCEPT AND MEASUREMENT OF VOLUNTARY ABSENCE

In this chapter we discuss the advantages and disadvantages of assuming that a proportion of absences is voluntary. This assumption seems useful from the viewpoint of potential management control of absence rates, although this is not the reason for our interest in it in this chapter.

We consider it important to discuss the process of choosing to be absent for two reasons. First, this kind of decision has a psychological interest—and if we consider individuals' choices, we do so always with awareness of the social context that interacts with them. In other words, we assume that within a given population, there will be wide individual variations, but that the nature and limits of these variations will be related to a social norm of absences. Second, there is a methodological interest: voluntary choice, as the notion is developed theoretically, also has to be based on empirical measures. In other words, we will attempt to specify the methods that may differentiate (at least partially) voluntary and involuntary absences.

In the study of absence from work, the concept of voluntary absence or absenteeism has often been utilized. For example, medical studies have drawn distinctions between absence due to physical or mental inability to perform work duties and absence for any other (often unspecified) reason (Gordon, Emerson, and Pugh 1959). Absence without a medical certificate (Hill and Trist 1955) and "other reasons" absence (Schenet 1945) have been utilized frequently as measures of voluntary absence. While the contrast between voluntary and involuntary absence has an appealing common-sense basis, in practice the distinction becomes confused with other factors, all of them evaluative—such as the notion of absences that are "acceptable" or "irresponsible."

Absence as voluntary withdrawal was discussed by Hill and Trist (1953; 1962) in their classic studies, giving full attention to the psychological implications of absences. There are other, similar treatments. Knox (1961) and Ås (1962) discuss "barriers to attendance," and postulate a continuum from insuperable barriers to no barrier at all. The approach used by Vroom (1964) is based on an instrumental concept of absence behavior that seeks to account for absence in terms of its perceived result or outcome. Voluntary absences are viewed as outcome-dependent (instrumental), and may be contrasted with absences that are the result of influences and events predetermining their occurrence. Such "determined" absences correspond to involuntary absence, whereas instrumental absences may be chosen by the individual in a trade-off with the organization. This explanation is similar to the one that we argue in this book, although we place considerably more emphasis on the group pattern of social exchange in the empirical analysis and the theory that we develop.

In their thorough review Steers and Rhodes (1978) distinguish between voluntary absences and absences where the individual does not exercise choice. These authors identify at least three kinds of unavoidable factors that lead to absences: illness and accidents, family responsibilities, and transportation problems (distance from work, weather, availability of public transport).

The medical notion of physical incapacity, considering an incapacitating disease as outside the realm of choice behavior (compare the idea of insuperable "barriers to attendance" favored by Knox 1961), is questionable because certain illnesses are psychosomatic and minor accidents may be "chosen," especially in terms of their timing, as a means to withdrawal (Hill and Trist 1955; 1962). Furthermore, in the case of illness, persons may decide that their physical state is such that they cannot go to work, and subsequently they seek a medical certificate to legitimize that decision. Many conditions, such as backache or gastrointestinal complaints, are often impossible to confirm medically within the usual context of general medical practice; it has been estimated that around one-third of diagnoses are based entirely on the verbal report of patients (see Chapter 1).

Some social scientists have defined voluntary absence in managerial terms. Thus, Behrend (1959) defines absenteeism as "the practice of workers failing to report to work on some slight excuse or other, or none at all," but leaves unanswered the question of who is to judge whether certain absences are "excusable" or not.

Managerial assessments of absence often relate to the interpretation of excuses for absence, and this problem of course underlies the definition utilized by Behrend. There may also be a managerial assumption concerning absences that can (and that cannot) be controlled. This notion may touch on the question of whether the absence was caused by invariable factors. Some "unchosen" absences, resulting from factors in the working environment, may actually be the most amenable to control—for example, by the elimination of safety hazards. On the other hand, attempting to control occasional short ("chosen") absences may be undesirable (or impracticable) from management's point of view. Sometimes supervisory surveillance may be used to reduce absences, monitoring the excuses given and invoking disciplinary action such as "warning" and "final warning" procedures. Of course, the whole issue of managerial controls is problematical (we shall return to it in Chapter 9), and they cannot be considered in the abstract, without admitting possibilities of other, unintended consequences, such as reactions by trade unions.

Managerial studies have not been unidirectional in their areas of interest. They have investigated the consequences of absences for manpower planning; for recruitment, overmanning, and other coping strategies; or for costs (Mirvis and Lawler 1977). Most frequently, managerial studies have sought indicators of absences that are particularly amenable to control (Plummer 1960; Seatter 1961; Mikalachki, 1975; Mikalanchki and Chapple 1977), or have tried to identify those correlated factors that may be amenable to managerial control. But in both medical and managerial studies, the statistic most usually employed has been time lost, and this measure, since it is biased toward representing long-term sickness (especially in the blue-collar industries), seems much more suitable for medical than management studies.

CHOICE AND ABSENCE

The operation of choices within a range of what is socially permitted is worthy of attention from social scientists, and the judged degree of choice involved in absences from work is important because it may influence managerial evaluations of absence. However, questions about whether choices are relatively free or restrained are difficult to resolve. Therefore medical, managerial, and psychological distinctions between voluntary and involuntary types of absence have typically been drawn in terms of a continuum rather than as two distinct types.

As we have just discussed, there is evidence to suggest that some certificated absence (that is, absence excused by medical certificate) will be voluntary rather than "involuntary." Buzzard and Shaw (1952) and Denerley (1952) observed large increases in sickness absence following the introduction of sick pay schemes, without a corresponding decrease in other types of absence; in one company the rate of time lost more than doubled in the 12 months following the introduction of a "sickness benefit" scheme. Jones (1971) commented that such increases cannot be fully attributed to "genuinely sick workers who prior to the introduction of such schemes were forced to carry on because of the economic consequences of absence." The extent to which chosen absence is disguised as certificated sickness is impossible to assess, and certainly such "concealed" choice must occur. Nevertheless, in longer-term sickness absence the choice factor probably is less than in other types, such as one-day absences. Absence estimates based only on total time lost tend to miss the choice component because these figures are heavily weighted by longer-term absences, especially in blue-collar industries where sickness levels are high.

It is important to recognize that choice is potentially relevant; whether it is, in fact, exercised is another matter. Assuming that choice is potentially relevant avoids the notion that individuals continually assess the advantages and disadvantages of going to work, each day arriving at a decision. The exercise of choice is a complex interaction of individual personality dynamics and prevailing conditions. An assumption of continual instrumental choice is not necessary. We need say only that some form of rational decision, conscious or unconscious, frequently occurs.

Choosing to be absent probably seldom relates solely to job incentives involving the motivation to work. When we try to account for the how and why of choices (to be absent or present), we must include the social context of norms or ideas shared by employees, and often by employers, about how many days an employee can reasonably be absent in a month without having a medical certificate. Thus, we recognize some consensus among employees and collusion between employees and employers. In doing so, we have avoided prejudging absenteeism in a pejorative way. Absences that may seem, to management, to be a means of avoiding job responsibilities can also be interpreted as providing an opportunity to meet family responsibilities and other social needs. Davis and Cherns make an acute comment when they write: "We could argue that our culture places what should be the community's responsibility—to get society's work done—on the individual, while placing what should be the individual's responsibility—to make himself available for other people who need him—on impersonal community organizations" (1975, p. 24). This comment has extremely deep implications. Of course, absenteeism may express a hedonistic, irresponsible attack on the work ethic—it may, on the other hand, be an answer to demands for child care or family care, and it may be constructive for the individual as a social being in a given class and culture. In other words, we cannot commit ourselves to a pejorative view of absenteeism.

THE "TIME-LOST" MEASURE

It is now necessary to evaluate existing measures of absence for their efficiency in capturing the operation of choice. As we have seen, studies in medicine have usually centered on the causes and correlates of absence due to physical or mental incapacity. This type of absence corresponds closely to our idea of unchosen absence. By far the most common measure used in this kind of study, time lost, is defined as the percentage of possible or scheduled working time lost due to all types of absences.

Some researchers, seeking to identify the psychological correlates of absence, have intercorrelated personal and psychological variables with a "time lost" measure (Schenet 1945; Hewitt and Parfitt 1953). Others have raised objections to this procedure (Acton Society Trust 1953; Behrend 1953), suggesting that alternative measures of absence may be more suitable. Nevertheless, when we reviewed published studies on absence, we found that out of 85 articles in which some measure of absence was employed, 62 used a "time lost" measure (Chadwick-Jones, Brown and Nicholson 1973a). All of the 80 firms that we visited in the initial stages of our research used "time lost" measures.

As was mentioned earlier, the length of any particular absence bears a strong relationship to the chosen/unchosen distinction. Absences that are "unchosen" tend to be caused by serious illnesses that result in longer-term absences: illness that removes the potential operation of choice is unlikely to be brief. Several writers have followed this kind of reasoning (Fox and Scott 1943; Acton Society Trust 1953; Yolles, Carone, and Krinsky 1975).

Clearly, however, not all short-term absences are chosen, nor are all long-term absences unchosen. In certain circumstances brief, unavoidable spells of sickness may occur—during, for instance, an influenza epidemic. Alternatively, some longer-term absence spells may result from choice, where a formal certificate of ill health has been obtained spuriously. These are doubtless in the minority, and while the length of absence and the choice continuum do not absolutely coincide, in general they are closely related.

To sum up, levels of short-term absences for an organization are more likely to be valid indicators of chosen absences, and it is clear that time lost is an inadequate measure of absenteeism, because it is so heavily biased toward longer-term absence, especially in industries with high sickness levels. The usual illustration given for this qualitative difference runs along the following lines: one individual away from work for one month with pneumoconiosis will contribute as much to the "time lost" statistic as ten men who choose to take two or three days a month. Other difficulties are apparent with this measure. Reports on incapacity for work have shown that sickness absence patterns vary considerably by geographical region. Furthermore, the influence of illness in certain age groups may be confounded with different regional effects (for example, the incidence of bronchitis among older populations in industrial regions). Since "time lost" figures are strongly influenced by such patterns, this raises problems for interorganizational comparisons across regions. Moreover, Behrend (1959) pointed out that the index can be distorted by lags in updating employee records. For instance, names of employees who leave without notifying the organization, may not be removed from the records.

It might be added that there are no standard organizational procedures for compiling "time lost" totals, even in Britain, where there are statutory requirements for supplying this information to government agencies. Thus the inclusion (or exclusion) of lateness suspensions, or even of "permitted" absence, in the "time lost" totals varies from one organization to another. Other anomalies are due to differences in the length of the work week. Buzzard (1954) showed that if working hours increase, it is quite possible for both attendance and absences to increase. Different amounts of overtime can also be destructive of "time lost" comparisons between organizations. These problems do not necessarily bar the use of this statistic for comparisons, but they establish sufficient grounds for considering its use as dubious.

Some researchers have attempted to break down "time lost" totals into different components that are assumed to correspond to differences in the voluntary/involuntary continuum. Of the 62 "time lost" studies we reviewed, 18 include breakdowns of total percentages by such classifications. Hill and Trist (1955), Castle (1956), and Kerr, Koppelmeier, and Sullivan (1951) distinguish between certificated and uncertificated absence, and relate the uncertificated or "other reasons" absences to the psychological concept of withdrawal. Others concentrate on the certificated component (Cornwall and Raffles 1961; Lokander 1962), and try to account for levels of sickness absence. The rationale for the use of noncertificated absence is that nonsickness absence is assumed to be predominantly chosen absence. However, there is no guarantee that the criteria for certification in one organization will correspond to the criteria of other organizations, nor is there good reason for supposing that "stated reasons" for employee absences will not vary in their meaning from one organization to another.

Accepting "stated reasons" and/or diagnoses at their face value would ignore the variability of expectations concerning legitimate reasons or excuses. It seems that absences are legitimized according to existing conventions, and game-like situations may exist between employers and employees. A standard rule in such games is that a medical certificate is a complete justification for absence, and here we run into all the biases and deficiencies of somatic definitions of minor illnesses that we mention elsewhere (Chapters 1 and 9). And there are still other sources of variation. The usual requirement of a medical certificate for longer-duration absences (especially of more than two days) may or may not be enforced. In contrast, some organizations threaten to dismiss any employee who does not produce a certificate, and vigorously enforce that policy. In these ways organization policies can affect the potential duration of "other reasons" absence.

FREQUENCY AND SHORT-TERM INDICES

A common alternative to the durational measures of time lost is a total frequency index (FI). This is based on the number of absences in a given period, rather than the total hours or days lost in that period. Frequency measures were used in 29 of the 85 empirical studies that we reviewed, but only seven used them exclusively.

The earliest exponents of this measure (such as Fox and Scott 1943; Walker 1947), arguing that the "time lost" measure was too heavily weighted by long-term sickness, suggested that frequencies could be a more accurate indicator of absenteeism (that is, of potentially controllable absences). Many subsequent workers have followed this rationale (Acton Society Trust 1953; Ingham 1970; Waters and Roach 1973; Johns 1978; Hammer and Landau 1981; in press). For example, Behrend (1974), discussing her study of one year's absences at General Motors (Scotland), makes an interesting comparison between "time lost" and frequency measures derived from the employee population. Of all workdays comprising the "time lost" total, 70 percent were due to certificated sickness; but when the absences were computed by frequencies of absences (irrespective of duration), it was found that 77 percent of all absences were uncertificated (of the remainder, 20 percent were certificated and 3 percent were described as "permitted leave"). Behrend concluded that the analysis by frequency "reduces the sickness bias and thus produces a better picture of the incidence of attitudinal factors in absenteeism . . ." (p. 8).

A derivation of the FI that has received relatively scant investigation is made by recording absences of only one or two days. Huse and Taylor (1962) named this the Attitudinal Index, claiming that these brief absences are most likely to reflect attitudes to work. We prefer to call it the Short-Term Index (STI), to avoid this preemptive assumption. Gibson (1966) believed that one-day absences are almost entirely voluntary, nonsickness absences. Froggatt (1970a; 1970b; 1970c) argued that these brief absences are "essentially voluntary," and investigated their relationship to personal factors (such as, age, length of service). He also analyzed different correlates of one- and two-day absences. Utilizing multiple regression techniques, he demonstrated that one-day absences correlated with lateness and with the number of two-day absences, but never with longer-term sickness (over three days' duration). Two-day absences, on the other hand, not only correlated with the number of one-day absences but also with longer-term sickness. This seemed to indicate that one-day absences were more strictly voluntary, whereas two-day absences had a greater sickness component.

In general, the STI approximates most closely to a criterion measure of chosen absences, in that it concentrates exclusively on uncertificated absences. There are certain drawbacks to its use. As discussed earlier, not all short-term absences are "chosen," so the measure may well be an overestimate of chosen absences. Conversely, some absences of three days or more undoubtedly have a choice component, and in this sense the measure would be an underestimate. The STI is also hampered by the fact that a small population over a short period of time (say less than six months) may provide few observations. Therefore, when it is utilized on a small labor force, the STI will tend toward instability and variability. This difficulty argues against splitting one- and two-day absences into separate indices, as Froggatt attempted, in all except very large populations over long periods of time. However, we suggest that the count of one- and two-day absences is potentially a powerful index of chosen absences, and we have shown ample evidence that this is so.

THE BLUE MONDAY INDEX

In five out of the 85 studies we reviewed, we found measures of systematic weekly absence patterns—that is, measures that reveal a greater incidence of absences on certain days of the week.

Behrend (1959) proposed a technique for the measurement of absenteeism based on weekly cyclical patterns. This index is provided by a count of the difference in total absence rates between Mondays and Fridays, assuming the usual five-day work week. Behrend argues that there is no reason why true sickness absence should vary between different days of the week. If, therefore, differences are observed between Monday and Friday absence rates, this demonstrates a degree of voluntary absence. Behrend produced data from 57 engineering companies (in the late 1940s) that consistently show Monday with the highest total absence rate, Friday with the lowest, and a gradual decline across the other days from Monday to Friday. The explanation suggested for this cyclical pattern is that motivation to go to work is lowest immediately after the weekend, since leisure has just been enjoyed and the prospect of another five-day work period is unattractive. However, the positive outcomes of absences will tend to diminish and costs to increase; thus, during the week there may be a steady increase in the number of employees returning to work.

Earlier, Moos (1951) had pointed out that there is a consistent statistical bias in calculating this type of measure. Thus, the Monday absence rate will tend to be inflated over Friday's because of absence periods that start on Saturday but are recorded as starting on Monday. Thus, any three- or six-day absence period that starts on Saturday will increase the Monday absence rate over that of Friday. Pocock (1973) has most fully investigated the statistical basis of the "Blue Monday" measure. He demonstrates conclusively that once allowance is made for the inflation of the Monday frequency by periods that could have begun on Saturday or Sunday, then Monday inceptions are much as expected by chance, and Tuesday is the day with an excess. He notes that in almost all industrial organizations, the actual numbers of new periods of sickness absence are, in fact, highest on Mondays, but argues that this can be explained by a purely random distribution of inception, since the expected Monday figure is 2.5 times that for any other work day. On this reckoning, the Blue Monday Index (BMI) is an artifact of the method of calculation rather than a valid measure of chosen absences.

Gordon, Emerson, and Pugh (1959) attacked the fundamental concept of the measure, arguing that, far from indicating high voluntary absence levels, a Blue Monday pattern may be evidence for high motivation to work. Their data show a tendency for sickness absence to start on Mondays, and this they interpret as indicative of high morale(!), since a disproportionate number of individuals manage to remain at work until the weekend before finally succumbing to sickness, consulting a doctor, and being ordered to stay away from work. Gordon, Emerson, and Pugh conclude: "Absences due to uncertified sickness will be sui generis higher on Mondays or Tuesdays than during the rest of the week" (1959, p. 238).

Behrend (1951) presented data from two German factories that failed to show any Blue Monday pattern. She explained this in two ways. First, the levels of unemployment in Germany at that time were higher than in Great Britain. Second, the payment disincentives for absence were far stricter in Germany. In a study of 318 employees in a British light engineering factory, Chadwick-Jones et al. (1971) found that Blue Friday was almost as common as Blue Monday. Such evidence suggests that under certain, as yet unspecified, conditions the BMI is not a suitable index.

It is therefore of especial interest that Liddell (1954) proposed an alternative formulation, the index of dispersion. This measure was based on the difference between the total absence rate on the "worst" (highest) and "best" (lowest) days of the week. Argyle, Gardner, and Cioffi (1958) applied this measure and renamed it the Worst Day Index (WDI).

The WDI involves the assumption that there is no reason for true sickness to vary cyclically, but in contrast with the BMI, no indication of which day or why any particular day will be lowest or highest is provided. It should be cautioned that, on the basis of chance, one would not expect the level of absences on each day to be exactly equal; therefore, the exponents of the measure must show that observed differences are not due simply to chance. However, in Chapter 5 we will show that the WDI gives useful information about systematic absence trends that is consistent with data for other measures of chosen absences.

COMBINING INDICES

Only two studies have previously attempted to investigate the interrelationship of different absence indices. Huse and Taylor (1962) intercorrelated four measures: STI (attitudinal), FI, medical absence, and total time lost. Chadwick-Jones et al. (1971), in an extended replication, added "other reasons," BMI, WDI, and lateness frequency, but excluded medical absence. Tentative support for the utility of FI and STI was found in both. We have confirmed these results in Chapters 3, 5, 7, and 8.

Up to now, very little systematic effort has been made to refine and develop measures of chosen absence. This may have been the result of poor conceptual analyses. In general, investigators have attempted to intercorrelate psychological variables with measures biased toward unchosen absences. The subsequent contradictions have already been noted (Chadwick-Jones, Brown and Nicholson, 1973a; Nicholson, Brown, and Chadwick-Jones 1977), and we have proceeded with the task of developing a variety of measures. It seems quite unlikely that any one measure will be adequate for the analysis of absences, a view expressed by Buzzard and Liddell (1958). Each measure discussed has methodological or theoretical deficiencies, but it seems probable that a converging approach using measures such as FI, STI, and WDI is most constructive.

The development of valid quantitative measures is, obviously, central in the development of explanatory formulations that can be tested against data. If the data are in reasonably reliable and valid numerical form, the theoretical enterprise can proceed more effectively.

Hitherto the theoretical analysis of absence behavior has been slight and few writers have been especially concerned with voluntary or chosen absences. This is why we have attempted to combine this concern with an effort to construct a theory of absence behavior.

5

ABSENCE INDICES

A STRATEGY FOR VALIDATION

We shall now analyze the theoretical rationale for a number of indices of "voluntary" absence. We argue that short-term and frequency measures largely represent absences that are the result of individual choices within the context of what can be called "alternative rule-following"—that is, within the context of informal "rules" by which employees collusively accept certain levels of absences as appropriate in their department, company, or occupation.

The evidence to be presented in this chapter supports the view that short-term absences are, in general, qualitatively distinct from sickness absences. The correlational pattern that we will discuss below shows a positive relationship between short-term absences and other measures of withdrawal behavior, such as the Worst-Day Index and labor turnover.

As we shall also see, the relationship between absence and labor turnover (leaving) is complex: high levels of short-term absences coincide with high labor turnover, but high long-term (sickness) absence tends to covary with low labor turnover. We will argue later that the latter covariation suggests the "compensatory" nature of longer absences from work.

Our strategy for validation was drawn from the work of Campbell and Fiske (1959), who state that two types of evidence should be sought, showing that a construct as measured can be differentiated from other, different constructs and that different measures of the same construct yield similar results. This kind of strategy has entailed examining the interrelationships of several absence indices over a 52-week period to discover whether predicted relationships emerged. We computed the weekly indices for each of the 52 weeks, and these provided the data for statistical checks.

We expected that Blue Monday and Worst Day Indices (BMI, WDI) computed for each of the 52 weeks should relate more strongly to the Short-Term

Index (STI) than to the Frequency Index (FI) and more strongly to the FI than to the Time-Lost Index (TLI), which is biased by longer-term absences.

RELIABILITY

It was possible to check the reliability of the measures by calculating the Spearman-Brown formula for stepped-up reliability based on the split-half technique. For each index in the 16 blue-collar organizations, the stepped-up reliability coefficient was calculated. We will now discuss these coefficients and their interpretation.

Table 5.1 presents the reliability coefficients for each index in the 16 organizations as calculated by the Spearman-Brown formula. The split-half method of assessing reliability measures the internal consistency of the absence indices during a given time period. Chadwick-Jones et al. (1971) compared two separate 39-week periods, but the comparison showed that differences between them were marked and reliability coefficients were low. It might, in fact, be unrealistic to expect stable values over two separate periods of time, in the dynamic con-

TABLE 5.1

Stepped-up Reliability Coefficients for Absence Indices in 16 Organizations over a 52-Week Period

Firm	Measure				
	TLI	FI	STI	BMI	WDI
A1	75	-25	45	-44	26
A2	68	-20	08	-20	36
A3	75	66	66	-13	-11
A4	17	46	35	-27	-08
B1	88	47	55	-20	04
B2	86	23	18	-11	-20
B3	73	51	36	15	55
B4	89	-25	06		
C1	97	28	37		
C2	94	39	10		
C3	80	65	36		
C4	95	75	75		
D1	97	66	66		
D2	92	00	-08		
D3	85	43	69		
D4	95	69	41		

text of behavior. Many factors might be expected to give rise to some interyear fluctuation in absence levels even if the populations in each instance were absolutely constant.

Let us examine the results of the split-half reliability tests, as shown in Table 5.1. The TLI is shown to be highly reliable and consistent, except in one organization (A4). Sickness absences might be expected to be consistent in their occurrence (except for epidemics) at the aggregate levels of the organization. However, the magnitudes of coefficients for the STI are also generally acceptable, with only one negative value (D2). FI has three negative and one zero coefficient; many other coefficients are high and positive. It might have been suggested, a priori, that the data for STI and FI would have been reversed, with STI appearing as least reliable because of weekly fluctuations. However, we cannot resolve the question about just how much fluctuation we should expect between one week and another, and we would need to know more about the general incidence of these fluctuations.

BLUE MONDAY AND WORST DAY INDICES

It will be noted that the Blue Monday and Worst Day indices were not calculated for the C and D groups or for B4. In these industries, with rotating shifts, rest days seldom coincided with weekends. It was therefore impossible to compute a Monday–Friday difference, and to calculate a Worst Day difference would entail drawing quite arbitrary seven-day divisions in a 365-day period.

In Chapter 4 some criticisms were made of the theoretical rationale underlying the use of the BMI. In addition there were empirical grounds for doubts about the universality of a Monday-Friday difference. Local factors seem to operate in each organization.

The overriding conclusion from the data is that the Blue Monday pattern does not hold generally. This is especially true of the three B group firms for which BMI was calculated (Friday absences are higher). In firms A1 and A4 Blue Friday is approximately as common as Blue Monday. Table 5.2 shows the Monday and Friday totals for the 52-week period and the number of weeks in which Monday and Friday absences were equal. Many of the weekly Blue Monday values were minus, and in B1, B2 and B3 an overall minus value was obtained, reflecting greater frequencies of absences on days other than Monday (Table 5.2).

Reliability coefficients were better, but still low, for the WDIs in the seven organizations for which data were collected. Again, local conditions are probably more important in influencing decisions to take absences on certain days or to avoid doing so on others. The nature of these conditions must be studied within an organization or within an industry. The evidence we have on banking organizations exemplifies the useful applications of the WDI in providing supplementary evidence (showing systematic fluctuations) to the other material showing that many absences are purposive (Chadwick-Jones 1978), as was shown in Chapter 3.

TABLE 5.2

Monday and Friday Absence Patterns in Seven Organizations
over a 52-Week Period

Firm	Monday Total Absence Higher (no. of weeks)	Friday Total Absence Higher (no. of weeks)	Monday and Friday Total Absences Equal (no. of weeks)	Total Weeks
A1	20	23	6	49
A2	28	18	2	48
A3	28	18	2	48
A4	22	21	8	51
B1	12	27	6	45
B2	13	24	3	40
B3	18	19	10	47

CONVERGENT AND DISCRIMINANT VALIDITY

In order to investigate relationships between the different absence measures, intercorrelation matrices between five absence indices across the six groups
of organizations (clothing manufacture, foundries, automated plants, public
transport, banks, and hospitals) for a standard 52-week period are presented in
Tables 5.3–5.15. The interrelationships were investigated by using the Pearson
product-moment correlation. A number of points should be made here to assist
interpretation of the data. There are degrees of cross "contamination" or overlap
between the indices that influence the size of correlation coefficients. In consequence, although we present the levels of significance attained by each correlation coefficient, very little meaning should be attributed to them in isolation.
Rather, it is the rank order of intercorrelations and their interrelationships that
is important. Also included are the means and standard deviations of the indices.
These provide useful indications of indices with high variability. In addition,
data are given on the percentage of shared observations between indices. It
should be noted, especially, that short-term absences comprise a major proportion of the FI. In one case this proportion is as high as 91 percent; in most of
the blue-collar groups the percentage approximates to 70 percent, while in the
banks and hospitals it is above 80 percent.

For the sake of convenience, the discussion will be organized around the six
groups (21 organizations), since there is considerable homogeneity of results
within groups. This confirms one of our main hypotheses: that there are patterns characteristic of occupational categories or industries. We shall consider
the industrial groups first.

TABLE 5.3

Matrices of Intercorrelation, Significance Levels, and Percentage of Shared Observations: Firms A1 and A2

Firm A1
(N = 145)

	TLI	FI	STI	BMI		Mean	SD.
TLI					TLI	12.2	3.2
FI	32*				FI	12.9	5.4
STI	−13	82**			STI	8.6	3.3
BMI	−30*	−31*	−21		BMI	−0.2	2.4
WDI	41**	51**	58**	−44**	WDI	3.3	2.3

*p ≤ 0.5%.
**p ≤ 0.1%.
Observation of first index as a percentage of the second
    STI in FI   68.0%
    STI in TLI   22.9%
    BMI in WDI 12.9%

Firm A2
(N = 563)

	TLI	FI	STI	BMI		Mean	SD.
TLI					TLI	11.0	4.1
FI	0.69**				FI	14.2	4.7
STI	0.25	0.70**			STI	9.8	2.5
BMI	0.02	−0.4	0.05		BMI	0.6	2.2
WDI	0.27	0.44**	0.60**	0.18	WDI	3.2	1.9

**p ≤ 0.1%.
Observation of first index as a percentage of the second
    STI in FI   72.6%
    STI in TL   11.5%
    BMI in WDI 18.1%

TABLE 5.4

Matrices of Intercorrelation, Significance Levels, and Percentage of Shared Observations: Firms A3 and A4

Firm A3
(N = 380)

	TLI	FI	STI	BMI		Mean	SD.
TLI					TLI	14.6	2.4
FI	-0.02				FI	16.4	6.1
STI	0.14	0.41**			STI	9.5	5.9
BMI	0.08	0.19	0.15		BMI	0.9	2.8
WDI	0.39**	0.13	0.40**	0.44**	WDI	3.3	2.9

**$p \leqslant 0.1\%$.

Observation of first index as a percentage of the second

    STI in FI   73.5%
    STI in TL   20.2%
    BMI in WDI   16.9%

Firm A4
(N = 152)

	TLI	FI	STI	BMI		Mean	SD.
TLI					TLI	12.3	9.4
FI	0.37**				FI	17.3	6.1
STI	-0.22	0.67**			STI	12.8	4.5
BMI	0.06	0.14	0.12		BMI	0.5	5.2
WDI	0.42**	0.02	0.27	0.06	WDI	4.1	3.9

**$p \leqslant 0.1\%$.

Observation of first index as a percentage of the second

    STI in FI   73.3%
    STI in TLI   14.2%
    BMI in WDI   14.2%

TABLE 5.5

Matrices of Intercorrelation, Significance Levels, and Percentage of Shared Observations: Firms B1 and B2

Firm B1
(N = 266)

	TLI	FI	STI	BMI		Mean	SD.
TLI					TLI	13.4	3.2
FI	0.41**				FI	9.1	3.3
STI	0.17	0.78**			STI	5.6	2.6
BMI	−0.12	−0.63**	−0.55**		BMI	−1.1	2.7
WDI	0.17	0.75**	0.74**	−0.79**	WDI	2.8	2.5

**p ≤ 0.1%.
Observation of first index as a percentage of the second
| | |
STI in FI   60.4%
STI in TLI   10.1%
BMI in WDI   11.2%

Firm B2
(N = 200)

	TLI	FI	STI	BMI		Mean	SD.
TLI					TLI	12.4	3.4
FI	0.46**				FI	14.5	3.6
STI	0.20	0.89**			STI	10.6	3.2
BMI	0.02	−0.12	−0.16		BMI	−1.5	2.7
WDI	−0.17	0.09	0.21	−0.20	WDI	3.9	2.9

**p ≤ 0.1%.
Observation of first index as a percentage of the second
STI in FI   79.2%
STI in TLI   14.7%
BMI in WDI   9.1%

TABLE 5.6

Matrices of Intercorrelation, Significance Levels, and Percentage of Shared Observations: Firms B3 and B4

	Firm B3 (N = 120)						
	TLI	FI	STI	BMI		Mean	SD.
TLI					TLI	8.3	3.1
FI	0.42**				FI	8.8	3.4
STI	0.28	0.75**			STI	6.1	2.7
BMI	0.18	−0.14	0.17		BMI	−0.2	3.0
WDI	0.16	0.68**	0.53**	−0.06	WDI	4.1	2.7

**p ≤ 0.1%.
Observation of first index as a percentage of the second
    STI in FI   67.8%
    STI in TLI   12.0%
    BMI in WDI 12.2%

	Firm B4 (N = 605)					
	TLI	FI	STI		Mean	SD.
TLI				TLI	10.1	2.1
FI	0.28			FI	7.9	1.6
STI	0.09	0.70**		STI	5.7	1.2

**p ≤ 0.1%.
Observation of first index as a percentage of the second
    STI in FI   73.0%
    STI in TLI   7.4%

Group A (Clothing Manufacture)

In each organization in Group A the rank interrelationship of TLI, FI, and STI is the same. In rank order the size of the FI/STI intercorrelation is highest, then FI/TLI. Examination of the respective standard deviations shows that FI has the highest variance in three out of four organizations, but the variability of STI is lower, confirming the reliability checks discussed above. Although the BMI does not show significant relationships with other measures, the

TABLE 5.7

Matrices of Intercorrelation, Significance Levels, and Percentage of Shared Observations: Firms C1 and C2

	Firm C1 (N = 580)						
	TLI	FI	STI			Mean	SD.
TLI					TLI	8.0	2.2
FI	0.34*				FI	8.1	1.5
STI	0.25	0.86**			STI	5.9	1.1

*p $\leqslant$ 0.5%.
**p $\leqslant$ 0.1%.
Observation of first index as a percentage of the second
  STI in FI   74.1%
  STI in TLI   4.4%

	Firm C2 (N = 250)						
	TLI	FI	STI			Mean	SD.
TLI					TLI	8.2	3.0
FI	0.19				FI	8.5	2.2
STI	0.01	0.87**			STI	5.9	1.9

**p $\leqslant$ 0.1%.
Observation of first index as a percentage of the second
  STI IN FI   70.1%
  STI in TLI   3.4%

TABLE 5.8

Matrices of Intercorrelation, Significance Levels, and Percentage of Shared Observations: Firms C3 and C4

	Firm C3 (N = 153)					Mean	SD.
	TLI	FI	STI			Mean	SD.
TLI					TLI	11.6	2.9
FI	0.47**				FI	3.3	1.6
STI	0.25	0.67**			STI	1.6	1.0

**p ≤ 0.1%.
Observation of first index as a percentage of the second
    STI in FI   47.8%
    STI in TLI   14.3%

	Firm C4 (N = 378)					Mean	SD.
	TLI	FI	STI			Mean	SD.
TLI					TLI	3.8	1.6
FI	0.27				FI	1.7	0.9
STI	0.06	0.76**			STI	0.7	0.5

**p ≤ 0.1%.
Observation of first index as a percentage of the second
    STI IN FI   37.8%
    STI in TLI   14.8%

results for the WDI do reveal a number of significant interrelationships with other indices. There is also a tendency for the WDI to correlate strongly with the STI, as could be expected if both reflect voluntary choices to a large degree. However, a few WDIs also correlate, in a similar range, with the TLI and FI, raising the possibility that some sickness absences are also part of a systematic pattern in which absences are taken on certain days more than others. For instance, there might be a tendency for sickness absences to be taken on days next to the weekend.

Group B (Foundries)

Similar patterns of interrelationships emerge for the organizations in Group B. The relative magnitudes of correlations between TLI, FI, and STI are identical. The sharp fluctuations of the BMI correlations with other indices are very noticeable (see in particular B1). The performance of WDI is, however, rather different. In B2 there are no significant intercorrelations, but in B1 and B3 the WDI correlates highly with FI, slightly less so with STI, and very little with TLI. This suggests that in these two instances the WDI is based on brief, nonsickness

TABLE 5.9

Matrices of Intercorrelation, Significance Levels, and Percentage of Shared Observations: Firms D1 and D2

	Firm D1 (N = 588)				Mean	SD.
	TLI	FI				
TLI				TLI	16.9	3.6
FI	0.16			FI	12.4	2.8
STI	0.08	0.89**		STI	8.4	2.1

**p ≤ 0.1%.
Observation of first index as a percentage of the second
  STI in FI   71.5%
  STI in TLI   10.6%

	Firm D2 (N = 198)				Mean	SD.
	TLI	FI				
TLI				TLI	9.0	2.6
FI	0.50**			FI	11.0	3.1
STI	0.42**	0.91**		STI	8.0	2.7

**p ≤ 0.1%.
Observation of first index as a percentage of the second
  STI in FI   72.4%
  STI in TLI   8.3%

TABLE 5.10

Matrices of Intercorrelation, Significance Levels, and Percentage of Shared Observations: Firms D3 and D4

Firm D3
(N = 157)

	TLI	FI			Mean	SD.
TLI				TLI	11.6	2.9
FI	0.34*			FI	7.4	3.3
STI	0.12	0.79**		STI	4.4	2.5

*p ≤ 0.5%.
**p ≤ 0.1%.
Observation of first index as a percentage of the second
   STI in FI   60.2%
   STI in TLI 16.5%

Firm D4
(N = 283)

	TLI	FI			Mean	SD.
TLI				TLI	9.8	3.1
FI	0.21			FI	7.1	2.6
STI	0.04	0.13		STI	6.5	10.4

Observation of first index as a percentage of the second
   STI in FI   71.8%
   STI in TLI 10.5%

absences, although, in order to account fully for the patterns in these organizations, it would be necessary to explore the local situations more closely.

Groups C and D (Continuous Process and Public Transport)

The data for organizations in Groups C and D (Tables 5.7–5.10) add further important evidence on the interrelationship of TLI, FI, and STI. Again we see that there is a close relationship between STI and FI, and only a small overlapping between TLI and STI. Indeed, with the exception of D4 the contrasting

TABLE 5.11

Matrices of Intercorrelation, Significance Levels, and Percentage of Shared Observations: Firms E1 and E2

Firm E1
(N = 208)

	TLI	FI	STI	BMI		Mean	SD.
TLI					TLI	2.8	0.7
FI	0.65**				FI	4.2	1.6
STI	0.54**	0.94**			STI	3.7	1.6
BMI	0.12	0.17	0.17		BMI	-0.06	0.8
WDI	0.12	0.47**	0.43**	0.03	WDI	1.03	0.5

**p ≤ 0.1%.
Observation of first index as a percentage of the second
    STI in FI   84%
    STI in TLI   48%
    BMI in WDI   8%

Firm E2
(N = 386)

	TLI	FI	STI	BMI		Mean	SD.
TLI					TLI	2.06	0.7
FI	0.58**				FI	4.26	1.5
STI	0.49**	0.84**			STI	3.77	1.5
BMI	0.03	0.15	0.26		BMI	0.54	0.4
WDI	0.28	0.30	0.42**	0.13	WDI	1.10	0.5

**p ≤ 0.1%.
Observation of first index as a percentage of the second
    STI in FI   90%
    STI in TLI   53%
    BMI in WDI   5%

TABLE 5.12

Matrices of Intercorrelation, Significance Levels, and Percentage of Shared Observations: Firm E3

	Firm E3 (N = 72)						
	TLI	FI	STI	BMI		Mean	SD.
TLI					TLI	2.8	0.9
FI	0.14				FI	6.0	1.9
STI	0.30	0.27			STI	5.4	1.8
BMI	-0.19	-0.003	0.05		BMI	0.1	1.6
WDI	0.27	-0.13	0.25	-0.15	WDI	1.6	1.2

Observation of first index as a percentage of the second
STI in FI   91.0%
STI in TLI   54.0%
BMI in WDI   5.0%

magnitudes of intercorrelations are repeated throughout. As was mentioned above, data on BMI and WDI were not available for organizations in these groups.

The interrelationship of the TLI, FI, and STI is remarkably consistent. None of the three indices shows excessive variability, and thus there appear to be no disadvantages to their use for interorganizational comparison over yearly periods.

It would be overambitious to postulate convergent or divergent validity from these data with the precision that Campbell and Fiske (1959) would prefer. Nevertheless, the general pattern of the absence measures supports our assumptions about voluntary absence and its expression in the indices.

Groups E and F (Banks and Hospitals)

In the banks (E1, E2, E3) and hospitals (F1, F2) the extremely high proportions of short-term absences entail a degree of overlap in the measures producing strong intercorrelations (Tables 5.11–5.13). However, the WDIs in banks E1 and E2 do show the expected significant relationships with STI and FI, again supporting the view of the WDI as a useful indicator of systematic absence behavior (that is, the choice of certain days more than others).

Next we examine the correlations of these indices with labor turnover. Afterwards we will discuss correlations between the frequency of dispensary visits and absence measures. Before we present this analysis, we consider the theoretical relationship between turnover and absences as developed by Hill and Trist (1962).

TABLE 5.13

Matrices of Intercorrelation, Significance Levels, and Percentage of Shared Observations: Firms F1 and F2

Firm F1
(N = 919)

	TLI	FI	STI	BMI			Mean	SD.
TLI						TLI	3.2	0.5
FI	0.72**					FI	9.3	1.8
STI	0.69**	0.90 **				STI	8.3	1.6

**p $\leq$ 0.1%.
Observation of first index as a percentage of the second
   STI in FI   88.0%
   STI in TLI   53.0%

Firm F2
(N = 322)

	TLI	FI	STI			Mean	SD.
TLI					TLI	2.4	0.7
FI	0.79**				FI	6.72	2.6
STI	0.58**	0.88**			STI	5.6	2.7

**p $\leq$ 0.1%.
Observation of first index as a percentage of the second
   STI in FI   86.0%
   STI in TLI   48.0%

LABOR TURNOVER

An analysis was made of correlations between six absence measures, labor turnover (leaving), and dispensary visits in the 16 blue-collar organizations for a period of 52 weeks.

As was mentioned in Chapter 2, Hill and Trist (1962) speculated that new-comers to an organization pass through a sequence of adaptation. They suggest that, in the initial period of "induction crisis," the rate of turnover will be at its highest—that is, a relatively large proportion of new employees leave. Later on, remaining employees become settled in the organization and choose brief absences as a means of temporary withdrawal. For Hill and Trist both turnover and absences result from the inevitable conflict that occurs between occupational demands and the needs of individuals. Other writers have also assumed that turnover and absence have a common causation: "The problems of turnover and absenteeism may be discussed together since in some respects the small decision which is taken when the worker absents himself is a miniature version of the important decision he makes when he quits his job" (Herzberg et al. 1957).

This relationship between absence and turnover has received empirical attention. Lyons (1972) produced an excellent review of the evidence on the relationships and shared correlates of turnover and absenteeism. Concluding that the studies have many methodological deficiencies and noting "a hodge podge of conceptually and operationally differing definitions of both turnover and absenteeism," he found that of 29 tests of the relationship between absence and turnover, 16 were positive and significant, 1 was negative and significant, and the remaining 12 were insignificant.

Interesting discussions of some of the complex issues involved in the relationship between absences and turnover are found in Burke and Wilcox (1972) and in Williams et al. (1979).

The results of a cross-sectional correlational analysis of turnover with absence indices for the 16 industrial organizations are shown in Table 5.14. The turnover index was calculated on all permanent departures from the organization, irrespective of the stated reason, on a yearly frequency basis. Except in very large organizations with high yearly turnover levels, weekly analysis was not worthwhile because of insufficient variation in the data. For this reason a yearly index was calculated for each organization. The correlations are shown for the six absence indices.

These summary results show a striking difference between the relationships of turnover to short-term absence and to long-term absence.

The results uphold the hypothesis that short-term absences and labor turnover rates may be produced by the same set of conditions. The statistically significant results indicate that, at the organizational level, turnover and absence are related in a complex fashion. In those organizations that have high frequencies of short-term absences, turnover tends also to be high. However, there is only a negligible correlation between turnover and the TLI, which is heavily

TABLE 5.14

The Interrelationship of Turnover and Six Absence Indices
Across 16 Organizations (Pearson Product Moment)

	TLI	FI	STI	% STI in FI	"Cleans"	Mean Length of Absence
Yearly Turnover Index	.12	.35	.49*	.54*	−.19	−.50*

*p ≤ .05.

weighted by absences of longer duration. And there is a significant negative correlation between turnover and mean length of absence. Thus, in those organizations that have a relatively high amount of long-term absence, turnover tends to be low. These results suggest that long-term absences are compensatory in nature, and that they could even remove the necessity for leaving the organization permanently. On the other hand, short-term absences would give only temporary relief from the pressures that produce turnover.

There are some further points to note. The correlation pattern indicates that turnover could be the extreme result of the conditions that influence the frequency of short-term absences. To the extent that the TLI represents true sickness absences, we would also expect it to show a negligible correlation with turnover.

DISPENSARY VISITS

A further index was based on the number of visits to an organization's dispensary. The index was calculated on a standardized weekly basis according to the following formula:

$$\text{Dispensary visits index (DVI)} = \frac{\text{no. of visits to dispensary}}{\text{no. in sample}} \times 100$$

In all industrial organizations in the sample, dispensaries or surgeries were fully staffed and recording procedures were adequate. Many visits to dispensaries did not relate to accidents but to general complaints, headaches, or minor injuries sustained outside work. However, it can be argued that all visits to the dispensary provide the individual with a respite from work routine, even if only for 15 minutes.

TABLE 5.15

The Interrelationship of the Dispensary Visits Index and Three
Absence Indices within Ten Organizations for a 52-Week Period
(Pearson Product Moment)

Dispensary Visits Index	TLI	FI	STI
A1	18	-06	-05
A2	-44**	-26	-01
A3	-41**	-06	21
A4	-03	03	-02
B1	-08	-20	-15
B2	31*	11	08
B3	11	-03	-05
C2	00	-06	-09
C3	-22	-03	-07
C4	-13	09	18

*p ≤ .05.
**p ≤ .01.

The DVI was computed where data were available, in 10 organizations, and correlated with three absence indices, as shown in Table 5.15.

In 20 out of 30 instances the relationship between the DVI and the absence indices is negative. Only three correlations obtained statistical significance, and these were with the TLI. The one significant positive correlation, between dispensary visits and time lost, occurred in one of the foundries, where it was possible that hazardous and dusty working conditions produced both a high frequency of dispensary visits and more sickness absence.

The preponderance of negative correlations, although many of them are slight in degree, leads to the tentative suggestion that dispensary visits may reduce absences in two ways: somatically, by giving prompt attention to minor complaints, headaches, or small injuries before they produce absences, and psychologically, by providing occasional withdrawals from work pressures. In general, though, this evidence is tenuous.

The intercorrelations shown in this chapter provide a consistent overall picture. We may note especially the tendency for the WDI to correlate most strongly with the STI, confirming the view that both represent a pattern of "chosen" absences, with the WDI confirming the deliberate, systematic nature of such absences.

6
THE RESEARCH DESIGN

The following pages present the design and method of the research. Although some of this might have been added as an appendix, it has been presented here because the latter half of this chapter refers particularly to the questionnaire on job satisfactions, the results of which are discussed in Chapter 7.

Relatively few researchers in psychology and sociology have experience in organizational studies of hourly paid employees, supervisors, managers, and union representatives. In this kind of project, there are many demands that the researchers must meet in order to carry out the design successfully in collaboration with people in a variety of occupations.

Perhaps some of the reasons why more field research projects are not carried out are to be found in the difficulties and delays that occur long before the stage of collecting and analyzing information is reached. Moreover, in field research it is unreasonable to assume that there is one best practical method of data collection for all organizations; design guidelines given by textbooks frequently are unrealistic.

In this chapter we give an account of the overall research design, of the research methods, and of some of the problems that we encountered. We will outline the scope of the project, the range of industries covered, the selection of companies, the types of data required, and the methods of sampling. Certain requirements of design and execution were basic and essential:

1. A range of different types of industry was to be studied; information was collected from blue-collar and white-collar occupations in manufacturing, public transport, banking, and nursing.
2. Standardized personnel data, allowing calculation of an extensive range of absence indices, were to be made available for all the organizations studied, covering a period of one year. In particular, some guarantee of the accuracy of such data was necessary; hence the researchers themselves took the mate-

rial from personnel records in each of the 21 organizations eventually selected. The time period was usually the calendar year preceding the entry of the researchers: 1970–71 in the industrial organizations and 1977, 1978, and 1979–80 for banks and hospitals.

3. Access was required to the relevant employee records within every organization. The collection of descriptive and attitudinal data was not to be restricted, except for reasons of sampling or economy specified by the research workers. We assured each organization that information would be gathered only under conditions of individual anonymity—that is, names of employees were not collected and the analysis of large numbers would make it impossible that individual absence rates could be identified. The identification of particular companies has also been avoided.

We assembled data from six categories of organizations: three types of manufacturing industries (four organizations of equivalent size from each group); one group of public transport organizations (four individual companies); one group of banking firms (three different banks) and one group of hospitals (two hospitals).

In Britain the first group consisted of mass-production clothing manufacturing companies. The second group was made up of iron foundries and included organizations engaged in the manufacture of castings and similar products. The third group included highly automated oil, chemical, and plastics firms. The fourth group was drawn from public transport companies: drivers and conductors. The fifth group came from three Canadian banks: tellers, clerks, and other grades. The sixth group consisted of nursing staff members with a variety of duties in two Canadian hospitals.

TECHNICAL AND OCCUPATIONAL DETAILS

The clothing companies were engaged in large-batch, assembly-line production, and employed mostly females. After the initial cutting of the material, employees assembled garments in stages. A variety of skills was required on any one line, ranging from complex and intricate sewing to relatively crude seaming operations.

The foundry companies either produced single units to customer requirements, as in the case of heavy ingot casting, or batches of various sizes to customer requirements, such as metal components for the car industry. Skill levels varied from the highly skilled molders to unskilled labor. In general, heavy physical work was involved.

The automated process organizations in oil, chemicals, and plastics employed male workers in monitoring tasks. Job conditions in process industries have been described by Chadwick-Jones (1969).

We now had a wide range of industrial organizations that included assembly-line, heavy engineering, and automated plants, and presented marked contrasts in working conditions and job demands on employees. We decided to add to these a group of public transport employees—male drivers and conductors of four bus companies—thereby providing a distinctive blue-collar sample.

The fifth group, employees in banks, was included because of the relatively slight attention that white-collar samples have received compared with blue-collar occupations.

The sixth group, nursing staff in a general and a children's hospital, was selected because, again, they would be representative of an important part of the work force and would be expected to demonstrate the hypothesis that as a distinctive occupation with unique conditions, it would reveal a unique pattern both of sickness and of casual absences.

THE SELECTION OF THE ORGANIZATIONS

In the initial stages of the research, visits were made to over 80 companies in order to make a careful selection of the companies eventually to be included in our study.

First, methods of recording absences within each organization had to be reliable and allow us to calculate absence indices over a 12-month period. In practice, this meant that individual record cards were kept for each employee. In manufacturing industries it was decided to include only direct production employees, to ensure uniform job content within organization categories. For instance, if maintenance workers had been included, then job content between categories would have been confounded because maintenance operations have some similarity across industries.

In interviews with managers in each organization, information was sought in the following areas:

1. Details of the product, process, and location
2. Management and supervisory structure of the organization; size of the labor force; breakdown by departments, function, job content, and promotion lines
3. Hours of work; shifts and extent of overtime
4. Levels of pay by department and grade; sickness benefit schemes
5. Length and type of training at different levels in the organization
6. Union organization; joint consultative machinery and recent history of labor relations
7. Type of absence records and statistics; other information available on turnover and accidents
8. Policies in relation to absence rates; extent of overmanning and overtime to compensate for prevailing rates; management disciplinary measures or incentives

Thus, on the basis of this information, organizations were selected as representative of their industry and, within their group, as similar in type of process and hours of work. Small manufacturing organizations (less than 150 employees) were excluded. Organizations larger than 1,000 employees were concentrated in the automated process, banking, and hospital groups. Companies that had undergone major reorganizations over the previous five years, such as productivity deals that involved change of manning or plant, or redundancies, were excluded.

Within the industrial groups there was some variety of job content: for example, the clothing companies varied in the quality of materials used (heavy to light cloth) and the rapidity of style changes on production lines (from unchanging manufacture of heavy uniforms to the production of seasonal fashion wear). The foundries' products ranged from ingot molds and heavy castings to lighter castings and small metal components. Nevertheless, they shared similar features: furnace operation; conditions of heat, dust, and dirt; a low degree of mechanization; heavy physical work. The automated process industries had a variety of products from chemicals to electricity and nylon fiber. The bus companies varied from operations in small towns or large towns, urban and outlying areas, to operations over long distances throughout industrial and rural areas.

In banks both large (approximately 100 employees) and small (approximately 10 employees) branches were included. Size of branch was one factor that we took into account in our analysis. We also carried out a separate analysis for tellers compared with other grades. The hospitals were located in one city; a full range of nursing tasks was represented.

TABLE 6.1

Employee Samples from Six Occupational Groups

Group	No. in Sample			Total
	Male	Female		
Automated process	1,372	—		1,372
Banks	137	513	(16)*	666
Clothing manufacture		991		991
Foundries	1,215	—		1,215
Hospitals	50	880	(11)*	941
Public transport	1,226			6,411

*Gender data not ascertained in these cases.

Table 6.1 summarizes the sample sizes of employees whose absence records were analyzed in our study of the six occupational groups.

METHODS OF DATA COLLECTION

In addition to collecting data from personnel records, research workers distributed job satisfaction questionnaires to over 1,500 industrial workers; interviews were held with 488 of these and with 231 white-collar employees.

Personnel Data

It will be recalled that a requirement for selection of organizations was the existence of comprehensive absence data in the form of an individual record card for every employee. In each organization the methods of compilation of such cards were carefully examined. The number of recording steps between the first note of an individual absence and its final recording on the card was checked, and in two organizations procedures were modified in order to reduce the amount of paper work and possible inaccuracies. The remaining organizations all had reliable recording procedures for completing individual record cards. However, no organization provided satisfactory summaries of the data, and the research workers themselves completed this task. Although this was time-consuming (appoximately one hour for five cases), we could then be sure of standard summaries for each organization.

Data from individual record cards were entered on preprinted forms in such a way as to allow the calculation of group indices by daily, weekly, monthly, and yearly patterns. For every individual shop-floor respondent to questionnaire or interview, a breakdown of absence records for a full calendar year of employment (or less if newly engaged) was extracted. Employees with less than six months' employment were not included; employees with between six months and one year were included, but they accounted for a negligible proportion of the total. The breakdown allowed calculation of number of days lost, frequency of absences, and number of absences by duration. All absences from work, for whatever reason, were recorded; only holidays were excluded. No distinctions were made between different types of absence based upon organizational criteria (such as "with permission" or "with medical certificate"). The main reason for this was that organizations differ in the criteria used, and such differences would invalidate comparisons.

Thus, the data allowed the calculation of a number of indices, but the latter were not completed until all data for all industrial firms had been collected, again to avoid possible bias in the compilation of results. The indices calculated for each firm are shown below.

Weekly (for each week in the year—to construct trend curves and to investigate corelationships with other variables)

1. Time-lost absence = $\dfrac{\text{No. of employee days lost in that week}}{\text{No. of employee days planned}} \times 100$
per week

The use of "days lost" rather than "hours lost" is preferable, since it avoids the problem that overtime work will produce a fluctuating denominator with a stable population, and removes the influence of lateness from the calculation (see Buzzard 1954). For some public transport employees who worked a six-day week and nursing staff on a seven-day week, the figures were scaled down to a five-day base before comparison was made with those who worked a five-day week.

2. Frequency absence per week $= \dfrac{\text{No. of incidents of absence starting in that week}}{\text{No. in sample}} \times 100$

3. Short-term absences per week $= \dfrac{\text{No. of incidents of one- and two-day absence starting in that week}}{\text{No. in sample}} \times 100$

4. Blue Monday Index per week $= \dfrac{\text{Difference between total absence on Monday and Friday}}{\text{No. in sample}} \times 100$

5. Worst Day Index per week $= \dfrac{\text{Difference between total absence on best and worst days}}{\text{No. in sample}} \times 100$

It was not possible to compute the BMI and WDI for the automated process category, bus companies with a six-day week, and nurses with a seven-day shift rotation.

Yearly (to compare different groups and organizations)

1. Time-Lost Index $= \dfrac{\text{Total number of days lost per 100 weeks per 100 employees}}{N \times \dfrac{100}{\text{no. of weeks}} \times \dfrac{100}{\text{sample size}}}$

2. Frequency Index $=$ Total number of absence incidents per 100 weeks per 100 employees

3. Short-Term Index $=$ Total number of one- and two-day absences per 100 weeks per 100 employees

4. Percentage "cleans" of total:

$\dfrac{\text{No. of individuals with no one- or two-day absence in the year}}{\text{Total in sample}} \times 100$

(This measure is derived from the proneness concept discussed in Chapter 2.)

5. Percentage short-term absence $= \dfrac{\text{Short-Term Index}}{\text{Frequency Index}} \times 100$

6. Mean length of absence (in days) $= \dfrac{\text{Time-Lost Index}}{\text{Frequency Index}} \times 100$

The rationale for the calculation and use of all these indices is discussed in other chapters of the book.

In addition to these absence indices, turnover and accident data were obtained through personnel or medical sources. The format of the raw data varied considerably between organizations. Using turnover and accident figures, yearly indices were derived from raw data. No attention was paid to the causes recorded for any particular event. Thus, every accident that resulted in an absence of three or more days, and any employee removal from the payroll, for any reason at all, were counted. Two yearly indices were calculated:

7. Labor turnover $= \dfrac{\text{No. leaving establishment in 12-month period}}{\text{Establishment figure}} \times 100$

8. Absence accident rate = Total number of accidents at work that resulted in subsequent absence from work per 100 weeks per 100 employees

Attitude Measurement

It was decided to utilize both interview and questionnaire techniques in measuring attitudes toward jobs and toward absence from work. The interviews are discussed in Chapter 3; the questionnaire results, in Chapter 7. The job satisfaction questionnaire was a modified version of the Cornell Job Description Index (JDI); (see Smith, Kendall, and Hulin 1969). The modifications are described in the account of the pilot study below and in Appendix A.

Initially it seemed desirable to have a job satisfaction questionnaire to measure employee attitudes across all organizations. However, banks refused permission for any studies of job satisfactions. The efforts by some employees to unionize was given as a reason for this refusal by one bank. In two of the banks it was difficult to obtain permission to collect only absence data, taking approximately one year in one case and, in the other, fully two years from the initial requests and refusals. In the latter case an appeal was made to top management, explaining that the university depended on the surrounding community in many ways and owed an obligation to serve that community in research as well as in teaching. This possibility of serving should not be rejected by the community, and (it was argued) applied research should be permitted as one form of service, bringing community and university together and avoiding the isolation of university activities. The chief personnel manager then granted permission for the research, but asked that all data collection be done at the head office, without visits to the branches (in the other two banks we had taken our data direct from employee record cards at the branches).

In the hospitals, although the personnel department readily gave access to records, the researchers took the view, after tentative discussions, that a proposal to study job satisfactions would call into operation a number of protocols and procedures that, even if the decision ultimately was positive, would take too long. And, if the decision was negative, it might prejudice our access to absence data.

The JDI questionnaire, with its five subscales (work, pay, promotion, supervision, co-workers), had an extensive history of development and validation in the United States. Its format appeared appropriate. It was extremely comprehensible; it had a low verbal content, requiring respondents to indicate by Y (yes), N (no), or ? (neither/not applicable) whether each of a list of adjectives described a feature of their jobs. The total satisfaction score was derived from the addition of the five subscale scores.

THE PILOT STUDY

It was first necessary to check on the instrument's applicability to our industrial samples. From the pilot study there emerged a modified version of the JDI, the Job Satisfaction Questionnaire (JSQ). As a result of trial runs, a 50-item questionnaire was devised (42 items of the original JDI were retained). In addition to the five scales—the work itself, pay, promotion, supervision, co-workers—parallel nine-point Likert-type scales were appended to each of the five topics. As we shall see, the pilot trials showed that item-whole correlations were satisfactory for both old and new items. The results indicated validity and reliability in three ways: sample satisfaction profiles closely resembled the JDI norms; concurrent validity coefficients (relationship between JSQ and Likert-type scales) were of a magnitude similar to the comparable JDI data (between the JDI and "faces" scales); and the JSQ scales' correlations with other variables (absence, age) were almost identical to those obtained with the Likert-type rating scales.

The pilot study included both male and female workers of different skill levels. Two separate pilot samples were taken. In the first, 150 female and 100 male semiskilled operatives in a footwear factory were given a version of the JDI. The modifications consisted mainly in the deletion of some items that appeared to be confusing. The main criteria for item suitability were item validity or internal consistency checks, and redundancy of items within any subscale (for example, in the promotion scale "good opportunity for advancement" and "good chance for promotion"). In addition, care was taken with the balance between evaluative and descriptive items in any one subscale, and this resulted in dropping descriptive items following the elimination of evaluative items for other reasons. One danger with eliminating items from the original scales was that a scale of increasing unidimensionality might result (a common problem with certain validation techniques). New items were therefore introduced to ensure that the comprehensiveness of the subscale was not weakened.

Furthermore, an introductory page was added, explaining the nature of the research program, stressing anonymity for the respondent, and mentioning the approval and consent of both unions and management. Items were added to assess how individuals compared their previous job in terms of work and pay, and whether they believed there was unnecessary absence in their section and the plant as a whole. Finally, a space for additional comments from the employee was left at the end of the questionnaire, and respondents were asked to give their clock number, department, age, marital status, and length of service. The JDI was distributed in the factory and collected the following day.

This pilot study showed the need for further modification. Item analysis of the proportion of responses to each item (Yes, No, ?) resulted in the removal of items eliciting a high proportion of intermediate responses. Point-biserial correlations of each item to the subscale score indicated that certain other items should be eliminated because of nonsignificant values (p greater than .05). The poor response rate (40 percent) led to discussion with respondents to identify causes. The result of this exercise was that direct questions about absences were discarded because they seemed to be more suited to interviews. The overall length of the questionnaire was considered excessive by some respondents, so the introductory part of the first page was subsequently shortened.

A second pilot run was conducted in a modern factory engaged in the production of clothes and other similar products. The amended version of the JDI was administered to 55 semiskilled female and 152 male operators. Eleven new items had been added to the questionnaire; respondents were now required to check a Likert-type rating scale on their overall job satisfaction for each subscale, which was later used to assess the concurrent validity of each subscale. A checklist question was included that required respondents to rank the scale factors in subjective order of importance. This latter scale was an attempt to derive a total satisfaction score based upon weighted subscale scores.

Once again the response rate gave cause for concern, despite prior distribution of a letter to the entire sample, explaining the objectives of the study. The response rate varied across four shifts from 68 percent to 35 percent. The response rate for women was 40 percent. Item analysis was performed as before on the 52 items (of which 41 were original JDI items), and as a result two were discarded (p greater than .05).

The final shortened version of the instrument provided a range of attitude information in a highly economical form, and yet general enough for a wide range of occupations.

EMPLOYEE INTERVIEW SCHEDULE

Interviews were conducted with personnel at all levels within the blue-collar organizations. The specific topics concerned attitude toward management and union, average take-home pay, individual perceptions of the right to casual absence, and the pressures on the individual to come to work or to stay at home (from supervisors, co-workers, or family—these results are discussed in Chapter 3).

Interview schedules were devised from discussions with managers, supervisors, and employees during the initial visits to companies. For the white-collar workers, who were interviewed in their leisure time, a short list of questions was devised to discover perceptions and practices concerning absence from work.

EXTRA-ORGANIZATIONAL DATA

Observed peaks and troughs in absence trend curves often could be accounted for by local events, such as election days or school holidays. Data on these were obtained from a variety of local and educational sources by telephone.

RESEARCH PROCEDURES: FIELDWORK

In the industrial companies, as soon as the final sample of organizations had been selected, approaches were made to the regional secretaries of trade unions whose members were directly involved in the project, seeking their cooperation. In all cases, replies were positive and the secretaries agreed to inform their branch representatives of the nature of the project, its impartiality, and the assurances of anonymity for their members, and to request full cooperation. The branch representatives were to receive the letter from the regional secretary six to eight weeks before fieldwork began in their plant, and if any problems were foreseen, meetings to elucidate any areas of difficulty were arranged at once.

A two-week program for two full-time research workers was allowed for field investigation in all 16 industrial organizations. On the first day contact was made with trade union convenors and representatives, supervisors, and production managers; discussions ensued on the aims and requirements of the project. Assurances of anonymity were repeated, and trade union officials and supervisors were asked to inform employees of the details of the research project.

In all but two cases this system of access through contacts with regional trade union secretaries, branch representatives, and convenors was successful. The two exceptions were in foundries, and we removed these organizations from the final sample, replacing them with comparable ones. The cause of failure in these cases was a divergence of opinion between regional and shop-floor levels in the union hierarchy.

Fortunately, in the majority of cases no difficulties arose and the initial introductory contacts ensured a smooth program for the research team. After the initial discussions priority was given to the collection of absence and all other personnel data on the standard recording forms. Decisions were made at the same time that the sampling procedures for interviews and questionnaire distribution were established.

Sampling Procedures

In some plants decisions had to be made to limit the scope of the investigation to one main production area. For example, in the two largest automated process companies all records and data taken were specific to one production unit.

A sample was then selected for distribution of the JSQ and another, smaller sample was selected for interview. The basis for these sampling procedures varied in different organizations, with the overall objective of selecting samples that were as typical of a particular organization as possible—that is, by random sampling of employees within production units and work grades.

Methods of Questionnaire Distribution

Methods of distribution were not uniform across the sample because of differing in-plant conditions. In some cases respondents completed the questionnaire in a factory canteen during working hours. In these circumstances assistance from the research workers was required, but a very high response rate was achieved.

However, in the majority of companies, questionnaire completion was not permitted by management during working hours and a "take-home" distribution was used. Thus, procedures were developed to optimize the response rate. Distribution of the questionnaire was left until the last stages of the fieldwork program in order that the presence and purposes of the research workers would be more widely known. With "take-home" distribution, questionnaires were given to workers individually at the end of the shift and assurances of anonymity were personally provided; workers were asked to return questionnaires to the research workers at the start of the following shift. Late returns were either to be handed to the research team or placed in a sealed box in the factory or canteen. Respondents were reminded that they were free to consult their union representatives for further information.

In clothing manufacture, conditions for achieving high response rates were most favorable. Each operative had her own position on the line, and it was therefore very easy for the research workers to arrange collection of completed forms at the place of work.

Methods of distribution in foundries were varied: in some organizations questionnaires were handed out during working hours in the canteen, while in others there was "take-home" distribution. In automated plants the difficulties of a "take-home" distribution to four shifts constituted a major problem. It was necessary in some of these organizations to arrange for a union official to collect the forms and hand them to the research workers later. This procedure was not thought really desirable, and was avoided where possible. In bus companies where hours were staggered, only a small proportion of the work force was in one place at one time. That place was usually the canteen, which became the effective base of operations for the research team. Questionnaires were completed either on the spot, if shift arrangements allowed sufficient free time, or, more usually, were filled in at home.

Methods of Employee Interviewing

In all cases the research workers were responsible for the selection of interviewees, but the time and order of interviews depended upon the decision of the supervisor or production manager for that section. Interviews were conducted as close as possible to the place of work, in order to minimize disruption of normal working: in cafeterias or at the workbench where possible.

For white-collar employees it was decided, after our encounters with the opposition from banks, to bypass the authority structure by interviewing clerical and office workers wherever research students might be able to meet them: on coffee and lunch breaks, on the bus, or in their homes. The interview schedule was relatively short, but was oriented to obtaining insights into what the employees thought about absence from work and how much they differentiated between different kinds and occasions of absence; the results are discussed in Chapter 3.

7
ABSENTEEISM AND JOB SATISFACTIONS

The belief that frequent absences from work occur as a consequence of job dissatisfaction is widespread among both managers and social scientists. The notion has intuitive appeal. It "makes sense" to assert that happy workers will be at work more regularly and that dissatisfied people will seek opportunities to avoid going to work. The proposition offers a vindication for job satisfaction studies in the face of the repeated failure of research to demonstrate a reliable relationship between job attitudes and productivity (Brayfield and Crockett 1955). It also provides a rationale for employers who actively seek to improve the quality of their employees' work experience. However, the measurable contribution of job satisfactions to absences is small; the proportion of dissatisfied employees in any working population is always low, and measures of job satisfaction fail to represent the dynamics of work situations where employees who express high job satisfactions still experience overload or boredom at certain times of the week or month. Last, there is a logical flaw in assuming that job satisfactions are an "independent" variable and absences a "dependent" variable, because absence opportunities may well influence job satisfactions.

A review of studies focusing on the statistical association between job satisfactions and absences recommends some caution. From our examination of 29 studies reporting on the question, it is quite clear that inconsistencies abound in the methods and measures used, populations sampled, and results reported. Table 7.1 summarizes the findings of these studies, subdividing them into three distinctive methodological categories.

LITERATURE ON THE ABSENCE-SATISFACTION RELATIONSHIP

The characteristics of the studies in each group and the empirical status of their findings may be considered separately.

TABLE 7.1

Literature on the Absence-Satisfaction Relationship, Categorized by Methodology

Source	Sample	Relationship Found
	Category 1: Individual Correlational Studies	
Noland (1945)	466 blue-collar males	negative
Van Zelst and Kerr (1953)	340 blue-collar males	negative
Talachi (1960)	42 blue-collar males	negative
Patchen (1960)	487 male process operators	negative
Harding and Bottenberg (1961)	376 airmen	zero
Vroom (1962)	489 male process operators	zero
Gadourek (1965)	2,227 blue-collar males	zero
Gerstenfeld (1969)	148 blue-collar females	zero
Smith, Kendall, and Hulin (1969)	98 blue-collar males	negative (4 scales) and zero (1 scale)
Hackman and Lawler (1971)	208 blue-collar males	zero
Waters and Roach (1971)	160 white-collar females	negative (2 scales) and zero (3 scales)
Waters and Roach (1973)	197 white-collar females	negative (1 scale) and zero (4 scales)
Newman (1974)	108 male and female nursing staff	zero
Clark (1975)	62 female student nurses	zero
Nicholson, Wall, and Lischeron (1977)	95 blue-collar males	negative (3 scales) and zero (3 scales)

Category 2: Criterion or Contrasted Group Studies

Kornhauser and Sharp (1932)	200 blue-collar females	negative
Fraser (1947)	3,000 blue-collar males and females	negative
Katz and Hyman (1947)	1,800 blue-collar males	negative
Metzner and Mann (1953)	251 blue-collar males	negative
	163 white-collar males	negative
	212 white-collar females	zero
White (1960)	50 blue-collar males and females	negative (2 scales) and zero (4 scales)
Taylor (1968)	194 male process operators	negative
Ferguson (1972)	109 blue-collar males	negative
OPCS (1973)	7,998 males (all occupations)	negative
	5,072 females (all occupations)	negative

Category 3: Group Correlational Studies

Kerr, Koppelmeier, and Sullivan (1951)	19 factory departments	negative
Mann and Baumgartel (1952)	163 white-collar males	negative
	251 blue-collar males	negative
Lundquist (1959)	9 factory departments	negative
Ås (1962)	18 factory work groups	zero
Mann, Indik, and Vroom (1963)	24 factory work groups	negative
	28 company work groups	zero

1. Individual correlational. This category contains those studies seeking an association between attitudes and absence at the level of the individual. However, of the 15 in category 1, roughly half suffer the drawback of using only one kind of absence measure or summary "overall satisfaction" measures. In addition, the great majority are limited in scope by their reporting of data from a single industrial sample. Results are mixed, with significant negative and nonsignificant correlations occurring with almost equal frequency across studies, and across scales within those studies that have used psychometrically sophisticated job satisfaction instruments. In no case are significant correlations of greater than modest magnitude; rarely exceeding -.3 where $\underline{N} > 100$.

2. Criterion or contrasting groups. Despite their apparent unanimity on the inverse relation between absence and satisfaction, there are two considerations that detract from these eight studies. First, in four of the eight, no tests of statistical significance are applied to data. Second, the selective grouping of data create problems of interpretation. There is a very real danger that inverse relationships found by this method only reflect extreme differences between subsets of the sample rather than linear association between the variables, and that intergroup differences on absence/satisfaction measures are mediated by other characteristics of the work setting.

3. Group correlational. As in category 2, the results of these studies have characteristically been used, incorrectly, by their authors to provide explanations at the individual level—that is, to explain the causes of individual absenteeism. This procedure is incorrect because this type of analysis bypasses all individual variance by grouping the data.

We now propose to discuss these three categories and the studies included in Table 7.1, comparing some of their results and methods. With this as background, we will then present our own study and its conclusions.

Individual Correlational Studies

The general pattern of results from these studies has been to show either weak inverse relationships between the variables, or no significant correlation between them. Studies using the Job Description Index (JDI), possibly the best-designed and standardized job satisfaction instrument in the field to date, have generally reported significant inverse relationships on some of the measure's five scales. The JDI authors (Smith, Kendall, and Hulin 1969) describe correlations with absence frequency for a sample of 98 electronics workers. Correlations were significant on four of the scales, though at a very low level on the work and pay scales, with stronger inverse relationships on the supervision and co-workers scales ($r = -.38$ on both). Waters and Roach (1971; 1973) have attempted two replications of this work. In the first of these (1971), using a sample of 160 factory workers, the only significant negative correlations were between the absence frequency and people (co-workers) scales after the partialing out of job grade and length of service, and in both cases correlations were of modest size. In the second study (1973) two groups of female workers were surveyed, one of these including about three-quarters of the original sample of the earlier study. A small inverse relationship was indicated between absence and work satisfaction.

The authors' conclusions on their findings were pessimistic:

> These data suggested studies covering one time period at one organizational unit may overemphasise the saliency of satisfaction variables in predicting termination and absenteeism. (1973, p. 342)

Waters and Roach further make the following observation:

> . . . the magnitude of the correlations was of questionable practical significance. Further efforts to determine attitudinal predictors of withdrawal behavior without replication or consideration of situational and personal variables seem of rather limited value. (ibid.)

In a similar study Newman (1974) provided results that were rather less favorable to the absence-dissatisfaction hypothesis, finding that both JDI and a modified version of the Fishbein attitudinal scales did not predict the absence rates of nurses, but were marginally more successful with turnover as a criterion.

Other studies of this type have generally used less sophisticated measures, and similarly have met with little success. In a study of oil refinery workers, Vroom (1962) looked at job performance and absence frequency in relation to measures of ego involvement, job satisfaction (measured by three, scaled questionnaire items), satisfaction with self, satisfaction with health, and work-related tension. A weak association between the opportunity for self-expression at work and attendance was found, but in no case did correlations attain statistical significance. Hackman and Lawler (1971) found employees' absence rates were lower and job satisfaction higher where work was rated highly on the dimensions of variety, autonomy, and task identity.

Van Zelst and Kerr (1953) threw a different light on the topic in their study of workers' attitudes toward merit rating. This covered 340 workers from 14 firms, providing data on attitudes, job satisfaction (a single item), absence, lateness, and past turnover by means of individual self-reports. Factor analysis produced a number of statistical clusters, one of which was largely made up of people with good attendance records and high job satisfaction. Low lateness and turnover were also closely related. An important qualification should be noted in the Van Zelst and Kerr study: it supplied no evidence that the measure of self-reported absence was a valid estimate of employee attendance. Gerstenfeld (1969) used this type of measure but found no significant relationship between absence and job or company satisfaction, although absence was associated with attitudes toward bosses and working conditions.

Talachi (1960) attempted to "fill the gap" in empirical work on organization size, absence, and job satisfaction by demonstrating a relationship between absence and dissatisfaction. He reported a low significant association between individual scores on an attitude inventory and the frequency of less-than-four-day absences for a homogeneous sample of 42 factory workers. Talachi also found size and satisfaction inversely related across his sample of 93 organizations, but the empirical links in his chain of explanation are not filled; there is no direct account of how or why size and absence are correlated, nor is there any direct evidence that factors he mentions—status differentiation and division of labor—do, in fact, mediate the relationship.

A more comprehensive approach was undertaken by Gadourek (1965) in the Netherlands and by Noland (1945) in the United States. Noland correlated absence with the responses of a large employee sample (466) on an 86-item questionnaire, and found that "satisfaction with job" emerged as the attitude variable most strongly related to absence, though the actual correlations were small in size. Gadourek's study was the most ambitious of its kind in the literature; over 2,000 workers' responses on a 500-item questionnaire were correlated with their individual absence scores. Despite numerous multivariate analyses Gadourek failed to find any evidence for an association between absence and satisfaction. Likewise, Harding and Bottenberg (1961) found no relationship between attitudes and frequency of excused absence among American airmen. However, it is questionable that the "excused absence" of this sample is in any way comparable with the nonattendance of industrial workers. Finally, it is appropriate to mention Patchen's (1960) application of equity theory in a field setting. He found absence was predictable from oil refinery workers' feelings of fair treatment in their promotion and pay prospects, but not from actual pay or their estimation of promotion opportunities.

In essays on the empirical and conceptual status of job satisfaction, both Lawler and Porter (1967) and Brayfield and Crockett (1955) expressed optimism about the predictability of absence and turnover from individual attitudes. The evidence of the studies reviewed here is too equivocal to support such optimism. Where inverse relationships have been found, they have almost invariably been of low strength.

Criterion or Contrasting Group Studies

The earliest study in this category was Kornhauser and Sharp's (1932) study of women factory workers, which found boredom with work reported twice as frequently by women with more than average sickness absence per month than by women with less. Fraser's (1947) large-scale study of the factors associated with neurosis in industry also found that groups disliking their work or finding it boring had higher levels of sickness absence than those with more favorable attitudes, but the differences here were slight. Nonetheless, the Fraser study is notable as the only reported work in the literature that has focused on neurosis as a direct cause of absence. Fraser concluded that absence is multiply determined by work attitudes and experiences, biographical and personality characteristics, and extra-organizational responsibilities and behavior.

In a smaller Australian study White (1960) found high attendance associated with favorable attitudes toward the foreman and the job. In the British General Household Survey (Office of Population Censuses and Surveys 1973), respondents reporting greatest job dissatisfaction also reported that they had had more time off work for sickness and personal reasons. This sample included people from all geographical regions of the British Isles, all adult age groups, and all occupations in the Registrar General's classification system. It is likely that the relationship found between dissatisfaction and absence was at least partly caused by other mediating influences, but no relevant information is available (and there are no statistical operations holding constant or partialing out such possible influences). An additional problem with this study stems from some reasonable doubt about the validity of the self-reported absence measures.

Katz and Hyman's (1947) contrasting groups study indicated that differences in work attitudes covaried with absence differences between groups, although no statistical tests were applied.

Metzner and Mann's (1953) study classified the time lost and frequency of absence of three groups of workers—white-collar males, blue-collar males, and white-collar females—and measured their work attitudes through a series of dichotomous questions about supervision, wages, co-workers, and perceived fairness of treatment by the company. The Metzner and Mann study is notable for its finding that absence-attitude relationships were more marked for the frequency than the time lost measures. Similarly, Taylor (1968) found significant patterns of association between attitudes and absence frequency. Among a small sample of oil refinery workers he found that high-absence workers tended to have lower overall job satisfaction, desired a change in their supervision, wanted more job responsibility, and expressed greater frustration with their work.

Ferguson (1972), using interview data, was unable to find attitude differences between high and low "sickness" absence groups on any dimension other than pay, though he did find that workers with drinking problems were prone to higher absence.

It seems unlikely that variations in the type of absence measure used could account for all the different findings described in these studies, though they may have been an important influence. In general, this category of studies (criterion/ contrasting groups) has been more successful than the correlational studies in demonstrating an association between attitudes and absences. However, in hardly any of the studies of either type has the possible influence of second-order factors been seriously considered. In only one of the studies reviewed here, Waters and Roach (1971), was any attempt made to control for them (in that instance the factors were job grade and length of service).

Group Correlational Studies

The underlying assumption of this method is that absence and attitudes may be sensibly treated as group phenomena, whereas the other two methods usually treat them as properties of the individual. None of the studies discussed in this section make this extremely important point explicit.

Among the most competent of these studies are those by the Michigan Survey Research Center—Mann and Baumgartel (1952) and Mann, Indik, and Vroom (1963)—in which absence levels of small work teams, all engaged in identical or highly similar work, were correlated with attitudes toward such factors as work and supervision. Mann and Baumgartel analyzed the attitudes of a large number of outdoor work gangs in an electrical company, and also gathered attitude data from their supervisors and managers. They found that high-absence teams tended to have a number of unfavorable attitudes, including dissatisfaction with the job. Two similar studies were reported by Mann, Indik, and Vroom (1963). The first of these, a study of 24 highly interdependent work teams, found a significant negative correlation between group measures of absence (time lost) and satisfaction with supervision. The second study examined 28 groups of drivers, groups with low worker interdependence, and found a positive correlation between absence and drivers' attitudes toward middle management.

This result may be taken at face value, showing that certain managerial practices may simultaneously dispose employees to favorable attitudes and high absence rates. Ås (1962) derived the same kind of result from a study of 18 factory work groups: a positive correlation between absence and satisfaction. Kerr, Koppelmeier, and Sullivan (1951) examined the relationship between absence levels and a number of attitudinal and nonattitudinal factors across 19 factory departments, reporting a significant inverse absence-satisfaction relationship across the departments. Lundquist (1959) used interviews to collect attitude data, but failed to find any relationship with absence after correlating scores across a sample of nine factory departments.

In summary, it seems that most of the studies in this category raise problematical issues, with the possible exception of the two Michigan studies, in which the groups were small, interdependent, and cohesive teams, and performed comparable tasks.

ABSENCE AND "MORALE"

Several studies have sought an explanation of absence rates through the notion of "morale." This concept (synonymous with "group satisfaction" or "organizational satisfaction") has lately lost favor with social psychologists, possibly because of its ambiguous usage. Despite the variety of definitions, "morale" studies touch some important aspects of the social meaning of absence.

Some writers—such as Talachi (1960), Harding and Bottenberg (1961), and Kerr, Koppelmeier, and Sullivan (1951)—used the term as if it were equivalent to job satisfaction. Others have invoked the notion of morale as an intervening variable to explain relationships between certain organizational factors and absence. For example, Brodman and Hellman (1947) used "morale" to account for significant differences between the absence rates of various departments in a study of female factory workers. Hewitt and Parfit (1953), comparing the spread of "low morale" to the spread of infection, tried to account for higher absence in larger work groups. Other writers have used morale and related concepts in a similar fashion in their discussions of size as an important organizational variable (Cleland 1955; Indik 1963; Revans 1960).

None of these studies, nor those discussed in the previous section (with the possible exception of the Michigan researchers), attempted any independent measure of group morale. For instance, Mann and Baumgartel (1952) reported high-absence teams as more likely to be critical of their foreman, to express low group pride and solidarity, and to include individuals who did not feel "part of the crew." Mann, Indik, and Vroom (1963) found some association between groups' absence rates and supervisor's ratings of their relations with the groups.

This kind of evidence is of interest because it suggests that the social environment in work situations can be a significant influence on patterns of absence.

SUMMARY: JOB SATISFACTIONS AND ABSENCES

Our review, which has served as a background for the empirical analysis of the next section, reveals that it is not possible to establish more than a weak connection between job satisfactions and absences; the evidence is mixed, even confusing. A number of studies have reported significant inverse relationships between absence and job satisfactions, but there are others showing null or positive relationships. Even where the variables are significantly related, the relationships are invariably tenuous. Correlations rarely indicate that very little of the absence variance is predictable from job attitude measures. Thus, overly facile statements that "Happy workers are good attenders" must be based on a very selective approach to the evidence.

We turn now to our own large-scale study that employed multiple methods, testing the relationship across contrasting organizational settings and measuring the influence of possible corelated factors: employee age and length of service.

METHODS

The instrument for measuring job satisfactions, the Job Satisfaction Questionnaire (JSQ), was a modified version of the Job Description Index (JDI) devised by Smith, Kendall, and Hulin (1969) at Cornell University. The extensive procedures for modifying this instrument, carried out after two pilot studies were completed, are described in Appendix A.

The JSQ was applied to a sample of employees (total N = 1,222) from 16 organizations. These organizations were selected (after we had visited 80 companies) on the grounds of acceptability of the research to both management and unions and the suitability of personnel records of absences. The researchers themselves extracted the absence data; procedures for distributing and collecting the questionnaires are described in Appendix A and have been discussed in Chapter 6.

The 16 organizations consisted of four companies from each of four groups. The employee samples were as follows:

Group A—Clothing manufacture: 407 female sewing-machine operators on short-cycle, assembly-line jobs

Group B—Foundries: 242 male production workers engaged in the manufacture of castings in traditional furnace environments

Group C—Automated process: 303 male process operators in plants producing gasoline, chemicals, plastics, and power

Group D—Bus companies: 270 male bus drivers and conductors in public transport companies.

In the subsequent correlation of job satisfaction ratings with absences, we used the following measures:

Time lost: Total number of working days lost in a year for any reason (excluding strikes, layoffs, holidays, and rest days)

Frequency: Total number of absences in a year, regardless of duration (that is, the inception rate)

Short-term: Total number of one-day or two-day absences in a year.

As we have argued earlier, there are important conceptual differences to be emphasized between the kinds of absence that these measures represent. Nevertheless, there is almost always some measure of overlapping between them, as Table C.1 shows (for individual yearly absence rates) and as the intercorrelation matrices of Tables 5.3–5.13 also showed for the weekly indices of each organization.

RESULTS

In Appendix B we compare the JSQ results with those of the Cornell JDI. We also examine tests of concurrent validity of the subscales with Likert-type scales and Hoppock subscale interrelationships. In the remaining analysis, to be presented here, separate correlation matrices (all product-moment) were generated for each of the 16 organizational samples; the results from these are now summarized. Table 7.2 shows the frequency with which significant negative (inverse) and positive (direct) relationships occurred for each of three absence measures and the five JSQ scales in the 16 organizations.

TABLE 7.2

Summary of Correlations Between Satisfaction Scales and Absence Measures from 16 Organizational Samples

JSQ Scale	Absence Measure								
	TL			F			ST		
	+	–	0	+	–	0	+	–	0
Work	2	1	13	0	3	13	0	2	14
Pay	2	0	14	1	1	14	1	1	14
Promotion	1	3	12	0	1	15	0	1	15
Supervision	0	0	16	0	1	15	0	1	15
Co-workers	0	3	13	0	2	14	0	2	14
Total	5	7	68	1	8	71	1	7	72

Notes: Cell totals show the incidence of nonsignificant correlations (0), and positive (+) and negative (–) correlations significant at the 5% level on a 2-tailed test. The median significant $\underline{r}$ for the middle range of sample sizes (those with $\underline{N}$s between 70 and 110) was .24.

In the great majority of cases—211 out of a total of 240 correlations—there was no significant association of any kind between absence rates and the job satisfaction scales.

When the test of the null hypothesis is applied at the .05 level to this number of cases, we could expect, if the significance tests were independent, to find 12 of the correlations occurring by chance—that is, a Type 1 error, rejecting the null hypothesis that in fact is true, might be expected for that number. However, in these correlations the significance tests were not independent because there is considerable overlap between job satisfaction areas (see Table B.11) and also some intercorrelation between the absence measures, as Table C.1 indicates (individual yearly figures). The intercorrelational matrices also corroborated this for weekly organizational indices (Tables 5.3-5.13). We could therefore expect to find an even greater number of correlations occurring by chance, thus confirming more strongly the paucity of significant associations between absence rates and the job satisfaction scales.

The weakness of the relationship is further emphasized by the facts that the magnitude of significant correlations was almost universally low and only 7 of the 29 significant correlations were also significant at the .01 level, with less than 6 percent shared variance in most cases.

Among the significant correlations, the direction of the relationship was usually inverse (low/high); there were 22 significant negative (inverse) correlations and 7 significant positive (direct) ones.

Significant negative correlations occurred across the five JSQ scales, as follows: seven times on the people scale, six on the work scale, five on the promotion scale, and two each on the pay and supervision scales.

There was no evidence that any one type of absence is more regularly associated with job satisfactions than others; significant inverse relationships occurred almost equally across the three measures (the slightly inflated figure for positive correlations on the TLI included three instances from a single sample).

In Table 7.3 correlations between absence frequencies and JSQ scales are tabulated by technology type (clothing, foundries, automated process, and public transport). The relationship between absence frequency and satisfaction scales was no more clearly manifest in one type of technology than another.

The successive and simultaneous partialing out of age and length of service from absence-satisfaction relationships was undertaken to gauge their effect on the relationship.* From this analysis it emerged that of 29 significant correlations, 10 ceased to be significant after partialing out age, 7 became nonsignificant after removing the effects of length of service, and 8 after controlling both. The influence of factors associated with age and length of service, clearly of some importance, are discussed in Chapter 8.

The fact that results appear to cluster in some organizations (for example, 11 organizations accounted for all 29 significant correlations) suggests the existence of trends within the organizational unit. It also supports the view that the organizational (aggregate) level of analysis is likely to be more fruitful than analysis taking individuals as the unit of study. It is a matter of finding the level of relatively homogeneous work or occupational groups in which trends or patterns may be demonstrated.

Thus, so far as absence rates are concerned, organizational climate or ethos, supervisory policies, management control strategies, employee-management collusion, and occupational norms are likely to be much stronger influences than variations in individual behavior. Research methods must be used that capture and make evident the operation of these influences, as we have attempted to show in this book (see Chapters 3 and 9).

However, there is the broader question of why the analysis of job satisfaction scales and absence rates did not reveal any stronger relationships. It could be said, as we have shown earlier in this chapter, that this has been another failure, in a long series of failures, to establish the relationship of job satisfactions and absences. No doubt this failure is partly the result of applying relatively superficial questionnaire methods that cannot capture the dynamics or politics of work situations. There is also a deeper failure: that of assuming that

---

*Under a predictive model of absence, part correlation (rather than partial) would be the more appropriate statistic, although the analysis of the data by both techniques was found to produce the same pattern of results.

TABLE 7.3

Summary of Correlations Between Absence Frequencies and JSQ Scales, by Technological Group

JSQ Scale	A Clothing			B Foundries			C Cont. Process			D Bus Companies		
	+	-	0	+	-	0	+	-	0	+	-	0
Work	0	1	3	0	1	3	0	1	3	0	0	4
Pay	0	0	4	0	0	4	0	0	4	1	1	2
Promotion	0	1	3	0	0	4	0	0	4	0	0	4
Supervision	0	0	4	0	0	4	0	0	4	0	1	3
Co-workers	0	1	3	0	1	3	0	0	4	0	0	4
Total	0	3	17	0	2	18	0	1	19	1	2	17

Note: Cell totals show the incidence of nonsignificant (0) and significant correlations (+ and −)

the individual's job satisfactions are directly linked to absences, whereas social norms may in fact be much stronger influences.

But there are many aspects of absenteeism that remain to be explored—for example, the operation of individual differences and variation within the normative patterns of a particular social context. We need to examine more thoroughly the size and nature of absence-free minorities in occupational groups, since in Chapter 3 we have already demonstrated that there are very great differences between occupations. These (hitherto relatively neglected) differences may also throw into confusion the traditional methodological approach by correlational methods. Hammer and Landau (1981) draw attention to the presence of a large proportion of zero values in some absence distributions—that is, the presence in some samples of many absence-free employees. Because the sample distributions are often markedly positively skewed, or have relatively few with really high absence frequencies, assumptions of homogeneity of variance (homoscedasticity) that are required for correlation methods cannot be maintained. This issue will be discussed again in Chapter 9.

8

ABSENTEEISM AND
PERSONAL CHARACTERISTICS

In this chapter we analyze evidence taken from the survey of 1,222 blue-collar workers and 1,302 bank employees and nursing staff, concerning the connection between absence from work, age, and length of service.

We will first present a summary of previous empirical studies and note some interesting conflicts in the reported results—depending on whether the research methods used were correlational (one point in time) analyses or consisted of longitudinal follow-up checks on employee samples over extended periods.

AGE AND ABSENCE

Arguments in favor of the merits of older workers are well known (Heron 1960), although the evidence suggests that much depends on the nature of the tasks involved. Porter and Steers's (1973) review of the literature on absence and turnover favored a rather pessimistic view: "Absenteeism may well be directly related to [age], although . . . relationships are probably weak" (pp. 164–65). But this conclusion was based on only three empirical studies: two relating the age and absence of male employees longitudinally, and one looking cross-sectionally at female age-absence relationships. It can be argued that, to establish the empirical status of the relationship, it would be necessary to distinguish between such studies in at least three ways: by sex of sample, by type of absence measure, and by design employed.

The results of 28 cross-sectional studies (dating from 1945 to 1976) are tabulated below according to the first two of these criteria (Table 8.1).

As for the third criterion (design), the two longitudinal studies cited by Porter and Steers are the only ones of their kind in the literature, and will be described separately.

The cross-sectional studies represented in Table 8.1 are divided into two categories: those that relate more to sickness and accidents (A-type), and those

TABLE 8.1

Relationship Between Age and Different Absence Types for Male and Female Employees, as Shown in 28 Published Studies

Sex of Sample	Nature of Relationship*				
	Positive	Negative	U-Curved	∩-Curved	Zero
A-Type Absence					
Male	10	5	5	1	5
Female	2	3	0	2	8
B-Type Absence					
Male	0	15	2	1	4
Female	2	5	1	3	1

*Cell totals show the number of studies that have reported data describing each type of relationship between the variables.

that relate to "voluntary," casual absences (B-type). A-type absence measures deal with sickness, "involuntary," sanctioned, or time-lost absence. B-type absence measures focus on short-term or unsanctioned absence (see Chapter 4). This distinction between A- and B-type absence measures was made by the authors in an earlier publication (Chadwick-Jones, Brown, and Nicholson 1973b), although we should caution that there is some arbitrariness in these labels. Table 8.1 reveals differences between male and female samples in the age-absence relationship. First, the table shows that B-type absence is usually inversely related to age (fewer absences with increasing age), and that this tendency is more distinct for male than for female employees. Second, positive relationships between age and A-type absence (especially absences of longer duration) are predominant for male samples. This fits the plausible assumption that longer sickness absences increase with age. However, for A-type absences other relationships (inverse, curvilinear, zero) are by no means rare. Results are more ambiguous for the women workers' samples with regard to both kinds of absence measures, but they confirm a clearer trend for male workers of fewer but longer absences with increasing age.

This generalization is contradicted by the findings of two longitudinal studies (Cooper and Payne 1965; de la Mare and Sergean 1961), which were referred to in Porter and Steers's review. These traced absence trends of groups of workers over periods of between 9 and 30 years from the time of their recruitment. Both studies found increases in the duration of absences, with no decreases in frequency. Furthermore, Cooper and Payne actually found that absence frequency increased with age. There are difficulties in the interpretation of this because of the possible influence of factors such as changes in current notions of a justifiable level of absence and lowered thresholds (over a period of decades) in what is held to be an excusable illness. The period of these studies probably coincided with general changes in attitudes toward work and norms concerning health standards, as revealed in increasing welfare benefits, more stringent criteria of fitness, and greater concern for safety at work. In sum, the study of age and absenteeism is likely to be confounded by such factors as these in prolonged longitudinal designs.

HYPOTHETICAL RELATIONSHIPS

The evidence of previous studies, as was seen in Table 8.1, suggests that we should expect less absenteeism among older employees. Why this should be so is largely a matter for speculation, although it is probable that older workers have greater attachment to their jobs and may be enured to negative features (Chadwick-Jones 1969). It is also plausible that besides being more settled into work routines and time schedules, older people may participate less in leisure groups, and may have fewer outside social activities and a smaller number of friends. Nor can other speculative possibilities be ignored. For example, if absences are a form of collusive reaction to fixed hourly schedules or to oppressive working conditions, this reaction may be found at its strongest among younger employees.

Clearly, we expect the effects of long-term employment to be similar and to be closely associated with age effects. We will analyze this association in the remainder of this chapter.

There is already quite convincing material available to support the hypothesis that long-service employees are likely to have lower absence rates. For instance, Martin (1971) showed a tendency for "leavers" to have higher absence rates than matched groups of "stayers," and to have more absences in the period immediately before quitting their jobs (Burke and Wilcox 1972). The suggestion here is that longer-service employees as a group have relatively fewer potential "leavers" among them, and therefore should have fewer absences. Other studies (Baumgartel and Sobol 1959; Knox 1961; Behrend 1959) indicate a fairly consistent pattern of high absence frequency among both male and female short-service employees. However, short-service employees are also likely to be younger.

With these speculations all pointing to a decrease in absence frequency among older, longer-service employees, we can examine the results yielded by our analysis of three absence measures (time-lost, frequency, short-term) in relation to age and length of service of 1,222 blue-collar employees (respondents to the JSQ), and of 215 bank employees and 825 nurses (Canadian samples). One bank would not divulge ages of employees, thus reducing the total sample to 215 for both age and length of service, although we were able to include all 583 for length of service only.

TABLE 8.2

Correlations Between Age, Length of Service, and Absences:
Zero-Order, Partial, and Multiple Correlations for Six Occupational Groups

Sample Code No.	N	Absence Measure	r_{13}[a]	$r_{13.2}$[b]	r_{23}[c]	$r_{23.1}$[d]	R_{123}[e]
			A: Clothing Manufacture (female)				
A1	145	TL	.05	.05	-.11	.07	.16
		F	.19*	.14	-.08	-.05	.27**
		ST	.20*	.12	.01	.01	.22*
A2	65	TL	.18	.21	-.09	-.14	.23
		F	.15	.18	-.14	-.18	.24
		ST	.12	.15	-.12	-.15	.20
A3	96	TL	-.03	.11	-.16	-.19	.19
		F	-.27*	-.18	-.21*	-.04	.27*
		ST	-.30**	-.23*	-.20*	-.01	.30**
A4	101	TL	-.12	-.12	.03	.07	.14
		F	-.12	-.09	-.13	-.10	.15
		ST	-.09	-.04	-.16	-.14	.16
			B: Foundries (male)				
B1	102	TL	-.08	-.16	.15	.20*	.23*
		F	-.34***	-.28**	-.19	-.05	.34***
		ST	-.33***	-.26**	-.23*	-.09	.34**

B2	58	TL	-.19	-.15	.10	.16	.29
		F	-.37**	-.29*	-.24	-.07	.38**
		ST	-.34***	-.26*	-.24	-.09	.35*
B3	62	TL	.04	.14	-.14	-.20	.20
		F	-.11	-.05	-.13	-.08	.14
		ST	-.17	-.12	-.14	-.05	.18
B4	20	TL	.06	-.31	.22	.17	.32
		F	-.19	-.51*	.07	.38	.46
		ST	-.10	-.30	.03	.23	.23

C: Continuous Process (male)

C1	73	TL	-.18	-.16*	.00	.19	.27*
		F	-.25*	-.27*	-.10	.14	.28*
		ST	-.18	-.18	-.08	.07	.20
C2	61	TL	-.15	-.15	-.07	.08	.16
		F	-.48***	-.34**	-.35**	.04	.48***
		ST	-.43****	-.27*	-.33**	.01	.43**
C3	87	TL	.08	-.16	-.12	.18	.20
		F	-.17	-.14	-.10	-.01	.17
		ST	-.22*	-.19	-.12	.00	.22
C4	82	TL	-.01	-.11	.09	.14	.15
		F	-.15	-.20	-.02	.13	.21
		ST	-.10	-.05	-.09	-.03	.10

(continued)

Table 8.2, continued

Sample Code No.	N	Absence Measure	r_{13}[a]	$r_{13.2}$[b]	r_{23}[c]	$r_{23.1}$[d]	$r_{12.3}$[e]
					D: Bus Companies (male)		
D1	76	TL	-.07	.08	-.13	-.13	.15
		F	-.47***	-.12	-.47***	-.13	.49***
		ST	-.48***	-.16	-.46***	-.10	.49****
D2	63	TL	.00	-.11	.15	.18	.19
		F	-.41***	-.33**	-.26*	.02	.41**
		ST	-.46***	-.34***	-.31*	-.05	.46***
D3	58	TL	.11	.07	.18	-.06	.20
		F	-.38**	-.45***	-.28*	.08	.39*
		ST	-.43***	-.46***	-.35**	.12	.43***
D4	73	TL	.03	-.10	-.02	.18	.06
		F	-.55***	-.26*	-.33**	.08	.56***
		ST	-.54***	-.26*	-.31**	.03	.55****
					E: Banks (male and female)		
E1	158 females	TL	-.15*	-.07	.13	-.01	.02
		F	-.25***	-.09	-.24	-.05	.07**
		ST	-.25	.12	.21	.02	.10**
E2	100 males	TL	Age data not made available	-.07	-.14	Age data not made available	
		F		-.09	-.18		
		ST		.12	-.19		

110

Group	n	Measure	[a]	[b]	[c]	[d]	[e]
E3	268 females	TL	-.06	-.11	.02	-.09	.01
		F	.19	.03	-.04	-.18	.07
		ST	-.25*	.01	-.07	-.20	.10
E4	57 females	TL	Age data not made available		.007	Age data not made available	
		F			.27*		
		ST			.33**		
F: Hospitals (female)							
F1	600 females	TL	.32***	.24***	.023***	.04	.33***
		F	.19***	.16***	.12**	.008	.19***
		ST	.06	.07	.01	-.03	.08***
F2	225 females	TL	.009	.02	.02	.003	.022
		F	-.13	-.07	-.06	-.04	.114
		ST	-.18*	-.13*	-.08	-.02	.17**

TL = Time lost.

F = Frequency.

ST = Short-term.

[a] Age/absence zero-order correlation.

[b] Age/absence partial correlation (length of service).

[c] Length of service/absence zero-order correlation.

[d] Length of service/absence partial correlation (age removed).

[e] Multiple correlation of age and length of service/absence.

*p < .05.

**p < .01.

***p < .001. (All are 2-tailed.)

We intended to examine the degree to which age and length of service were independently related to these different types of absence and to reveal whether any parts of the age and length of service ranges were critical for absences. More specifically, we had in mind two hypotheses that the correlations might confirm:

Hypothesis 1: Absence measures tending to represent short, casual absences (frequency and short-term) would show inverse associations with age (for male employees especially) and with length of service for all groups.

Hypothesis 2: Absence measures tending to represent "involuntary" or sickness absence (time-lost) would show mainly positive or zero relationships with age across all groups.

Employee samples were as follows:

Group A, clothing manufacture: 407 female sewing-machine operators
Group B, foundries: 242 male production workers
Group C, automated process: 303 male production workers
Group D, bus companies: 270 male bus drivers and conductors
Group E, banks: 483 female and 100 male employees
Group F, hospitals: 825 female nurses.

Within blue-collar organizations sampling was confined to the direct production sections of the work force. In hospitals only nursing staff members were included.

The three absence measures were treated as separate variables, rather than collectively (as they might be in canonical correlation, for example), on the ground that although they ostensibly measure the same single phenomenon, absence from work, they in fact embody important practical and conceptual distinctions between types of absence behavior (as was discussed in Chapters 4 and 5). This has been shown empirically by the variability of their interrelationships, although short-term and frequency measures overlap considerably (see Tables 5.3–5.13 and Appendix C for intercorrelations of absence measures).

The correlational findings for the 21 organizations are shown in Table 8.2. Correlations between age and length of service and the three absence measures are presented. The table also gives partial correlations for age and length of service with the other held constant. It includes multiple correlations for age and length of service on each absence measure.

RESULTS

The results show that absence rates are strongly associated with age and length of service, and that the direction of association is predominantly inverse, with only scattered instances of positive and nonsignificant correlation.

It should be noted that significant relationships emerged for the frequency and short-term absence measures, with few correlations in all the samples between age or length of service and time lost attaining statistical significance. (Hypotheses 1 and 2 were confirmed.)

Second, age can be viewed as the major influence on absences. Although controlling the influence of length of service did attenuate the relationship, in many cases the partial correlation of age and absence remained statistically significant. In contrast, the significant associations between length of service and absence did not retain statistical significance after the partialing out of age. With a few exceptions, the level of the multiple correlations is equal to or larger than any of the zero-order correlations, which implies that there is some additional predictive information gained from the multiple correlation. However, that the multiple correlations are not greatly different in value suggests that age and length of service could be said to operate as a single indivisible factor.

Relationships between the variables were clearest among the male bus company employees, and least among the female clothing workers. These differences are likely to be partly a result of gender-related factors (differential commitment to jobs and to family) indicated in Table 8.1 and discussed in Chapters 3 and 9. The bus company employees were a heterogeneous occupational group, ranging from the extremes of older, long-service men with a view of the job as a high-status uniformed service, to the young casual workers for whom the work was a relatively low-paid but pleasant stopgap between higher-paid industrial jobs (information provided by interviews with a sample of 140 men in the public transport companies).

Finally, there was also variation between industries in the strength of the correlations. In certain organizations there does seem to be a distinct pattern of prediction, such as all of D group (F and ST), C2, B1, B2 and A3. This suggests that characteristics peculiar to the sample on organizational setting can mediate, facilitate or inhibit the relationship.

An issue of interpretation that remains is the theoretical one of what associations between the variables actually mean. What social and psychological factors underlie an association of absence rates and age? The psychological literature on aging suggests increased stability, expressed in the notion of greater attachment to a job. There is also the possibility of a weaker commitment to social activities of all kinds outside of work.

CONCLUSIONS

The results we have reported in this chapter are consistent with those of previous cross-sectional studies, and confirm in general the hypothesis that age is inversely related to casual, brief absences. Our results suggest that young, short-service workers, especially males, have a higher average susceptibility to casual absence, while relationships between longer-term absence (time lost) and age and length of service are more variable.

The time-lost measure also seems more susceptible to random influences (for example, accidents), and occasionally reflects the higher vulnerability of older employees to sickness. At the same time, in some situations, medium-duration absences in the time-lost category can be the preferred form of "voluntary" absence.

These results are useful in three ways. First, they show that when age or length of service is examined in isolation, the former more often shows significant associations with absenteeism. Second, they show that relationships emerge with differential strength according to the nature of the industry or occupation from which the sample is drawn. Third, they indicate that organization-specific factors exert an important influence over the association.

9

PROBLEMS OF ABSENTEEISM

In this chapter we first consider some of the methods of presenting absence statistics currently used in international comparisons. We continue with a discussion of the conventional time-lost measure, and raise some questions about the meaning of average figures. As an alternative to the conventional approach we suggest a careful analysis of absence distributions. We present research evidence on absence distributions and discuss absence norms. Some distribution curves approximate to a classic normative pattern.

The samples from banks, hospitals, and clothing manufacture consist largely of women employees: in this context we discuss women's absence rates.

Past attempts (or exhortations) to reduce absence levels, especially as reported by management writers, are discussed. The practice of "chasing down" malingerers or rewarding good attenders is examined critically.

Since our research material shows that absence behavior conforms to a social or group pattern, attempts to control absence levels should, logically, be made at the level of the group or social entity. Thus, reducing absence levels might be a matter for negotiation between employers and employee representatives of the occupational group or unit. This argument is developed, together with the view that absences can be part of a trade-off between employee groups and employers.

Finally, we return to the intriguing question of management collusion in existing absence levels, even in the face of financial costs. Our eventual objective, nevertheless, must be to achieve precise and adequate analyses of absences by an appropriate range of measures.

CROSS-NATIONAL COMPARISONS

Is it possible to make cross-national comparisons of absence figures? The national absenteeism figures that are sometimes quoted have defects deriving from the often unknown and nonstandard basis of the compilations. The general estimates that are available vary considerably in the ways they are calculated—that is, in the rules that are applied for inclusion or exclusion of material. In some cases the figures include all long-term sickness and, in others, what they include is obscure.

"Absenteeism" or "unscheduled" absence from work is probably recognized as a management problem in all industrialized countries because of its appearance in industrial budgets as a very large cost item. Grossman (1978) expresses the management view that "Absenteeism is a cost-disruption problem."

Part of the cost comes from the necessity of finding employees as substitutes and having them available to avoid the disruption that unplanned-for absences would otherwise cause. As we have emphasized, the absences likely to cause most disruption are short, unforeseen ones. Yet, these short absences (often of one or two days) are not identified in the overall summation of total days lost that is the usual economic statistic provided in national and organizational surveys.

Absenteeism is acknowledged as a problem wherever there are fixed work schedules—in Europe, Asia, America, and Africa—and irrespective of ideological differences in these societies.

A number of writers in the United States have discussed absenteeism, not only as a large cost item nationally but also as an increasing problem.

In Britain, where there is a statutory obligation on industrial and commercial companies to supply information on time lost due to absence, analysis of trends since World War II shows a steady rise since the early 1960s. Taylor (1974) cites for the year ending June 30, 1972, the total medically certified incapacity for the entire population: 324 million days. He points out that there are certain defects in such very general statistical summaries—for example, the sickness benefit figures include all those who are permanently disabled until they reach pensionable age (they incurred almost one-third of the days lost). However, in comparison with these data, Canadian estimates—for example, by the Ontario government survey (Robertson and Humphreys 1978), are partial, incomplete, and, one suspects, subject to similar but unstated limitations.

Taylor (1974) notes that the Post Office in Britain has kept records of all absences for many years, and that these show a substantial rise in the postwar years, with the steepest rise occurring between 1949 and 1953. Taylor makes this general statement: "A higher proportion of the working population is now taking time off work attributed to incapacity and those that do so are taking more spells than used to be the case. . . . The prospects for the future appear to be poor" (p. 317).

Government agencies rely for their absence estimates on statistics based on days or hours out of the total work days scheduled. These estimates are very heavily weighted by days lost through longer sickness absences. The U.S. Bureau of National Affairs survey of 1974 was an exception to this, since it excluded absences of more than four days' duration. However, in general it can justifiably be assumed that current estimates are composed of a large proportion of absences due to unavoidable sickness. The extent of this proportion is not ascertainable in any way from the current forms in which statistics are compiled. Measures that exclude longer-term sicknesses would certainly go part of the way toward identifying absenteeism rates. As the U.S. Labor Department (1974) suggests, once an absence is known to be a long-term one, it should not come under the heading "unscheduled absence"—it is no longer disruptive. In Britain, Taylor estimates that 80 percent of all sickness absences might be genuinely the result of incapacitating medical problems, but that as much as 20 percent might not be.

Another important point to note is that the sample of industries from which annual absence figures are estimated is likely to be unrepresentative, and thus inadequate. The majority of companies appear not to compile absence statistics, and others may be unwilling to reveal their data to researchers. Some investigators have used indirect methods—for example, the study by Nickson (1972) based on supplementary questions added to the regular labor force survey conducted by Statistics Canada, although these are of doubtful reliability.

STATISTICAL RECORDING

Most companies do not maintain a statistical check on absences. In the Ontario Ministry of Labour (Robertson and Humphreys 1978), 958 establishments (59.5 percent) responded to a mail survey; of these, only 17 percent reported that they compiled statistics on absences from work in any form. A similar survey from the Nova Scotia Department of Labour (1976) produced a response rate of 160 companies (51.4 percent). The number that were actually usable was much lower because many forms were only partially completed or contained errors of various kinds. In this survey a follow-up was made, and companies not replying were asked to give their reasons. The majority "simply objected to fulfilling this request for information about their operations. Others indicated that the desired information was not available, or that assembling it would be too time consuming" (Nova Scotia Department of Labour 1976, p. 9).

In view of the somewhat doubtful foundations of absenteeism estimates, is it possible to ascertain to what degree absenteeism is more or less prevalent in different countries? It must be concluded that there is no satisfactory answer to such questions, because of the inadequacy of the national statistics.

In general, national figures are of limited usefulness because of the variations in compilation procedures from one country to another. For example, the British figures discussed above do not include absences of less than three days, while a U.S. Department of Labor formula for compiling absence statistics excluded those lasting more than four days. These variations clearly undermine comparisons.

LIMITATIONS AND USES OF THE TIME-LOST (SEVERITY) MEASURE

In previous sections of the book, especially in Chapter 4, we have drawn the qualitative distinction between longer and extremely short absences. The former tend to be a result of serious illness and unavoidable incapacity. The latter, specifically absences of one or two days' duration, often seem to express employees' decisions not to go to work. In practice, it is impossible to check whether "a slight cold" or a "muscular pain" is simply a convenient excuse. Thus, it can be argued that short absences are more likely to be under the employees' own control, resulting from their own decisions to take a day off. Again, it is by no means certain that longer-term absences are involuntary, but they are somewhat less likely to be voluntary. While some longer sickness absences will no doubt be the result of malingering and some very short absences will be unavoidable, it nevertheless seems justifiable to make this important, if rather fallible, distinction between the two.

Thus, the time-lost (severity) statistic is mainly of value for understanding sickness trends. It could also happen that in some industries malingering will take the long-term form, although there are good reasons for recognizing its limitations as a general indicator of absenteeism.

Whereas the time-lost statistic may be heavily weighted by long-term absences, the conclusion from studies in the United States, Canada, and Britain must be that the majority of absences are of short duration. For instance, Globerson and Nagarvala (1974), discussing data on "unexplained" absences gathered in a San Francisco company, indicate that the most likely period of absence is one working day. Behrend (1974), in a study of the motor industry in Scotland, shows that the vast majority of absences in a labor force of 762 employees are both short and medically uncertificated. She argues that counting frequencies rather than totaling days lost, provides "an indicator which reduces the sickness bias and thus provides a better picture of the incidence of attitudinal factors in absenteeism . . . " (p. 8). The advocacy of a frequency measure is by no means a new argument (see Fox and Scott, 1943).

In Figure 3.6 we saw that in all six occupations and across 21 organizations, with the exception of one low-absence organization, there were substantially large (majority) proportions of short absences (one or two days) in the total frequency of absences of all durations. In the blue-collar industries this proportion ranged from 60 percent to 79 percent of absences that lasted one or two days. In banks and hospitals these percentages were even higher: from 87 percent to 91 percent among banking employees and from 86 percent to 89 percent in hospitals. In both the banks and the hospitals the average length of all absences varied only between 1.5 and 2 days (Figure 3.5).

When, in our discussion of weekly trends (see Chapter 3), we examined the number of banking employees who were absent at the weekly "peaks" over the calendar year, we demonstrated again that the great majority were away for only one or two days (Figure 3.8 and related discussion).

AVERAGE FIGURES AND ABSENCE PATTERNS

A great disadvantage of absence statistics in national or regional surveys has been that they yield only gross totals of days lost, and give no information about the distribution of absences within an occupational group or organization. They tell us nothing about the size of the minority having no absences, or of the minority who are absent very frequently. As we have seen in the histograms in Chapter 3, there are very large variations in the proportions of absence-free employees. Figure 3.4 shows that the proportion of people who had no one- or two-day absences at all over a period of one year ranged from 6 percent to 75 percent.

From the 75 percent of absence-free employees in an automated plant, the range went down through 49 percent in a public transport company, to a number of organizations with only 20 percent, and eventually to 10 percent in banks and 6 percent in hospitals.

There are two main reasons why this kind of information is useful. First, the proportion of absence-free or zero values in a sample has important implications for statistical assumptions, particularly that of the normal distribution, and therefore might influence the choice of statistical operations on the data. In an innovative approach to absenteeism data, Hammer and Landau (1981) point to some alternatives for statistical analysis. Second, discovering the size of the minority having frequent absences has important implications for what we can infer about an absence "norm" (an informal rule that most people keep to) and a normative pattern of absences within an occupational group. In Chapter 3 we discussed the frequencies of absences and the proportions of absence-free employees in different occupations (that is, employees with no one- or two-day absences during the period of a year), and we found that these distributions revealed characteristic absence patterns. In some occupations there are large proportions of employees with zero absences or very few absences during the year. The notion of an absence norm has, evidently, to be treated with caution.

It might also be the case that while subgroups or departmental units conform to a norm, this does not show clearly in the organizational figures. Nevertheless, in banks and hospitals the distribution of absences does approximate to a conformity pattern. For example, in Figure 9.1 those with zero short-term absences constitute only 8 percent of the employees, and those with zero absences, only 6 percent. It can be seen from Figure 9.1 that 69 percent of the nurses in this hospital took between one and six short absences during the year.

In Figure 9.2 the absence curve is similar. Employees with no short-term absences constitute 12.5 percent of the total, and those with no absences of any duration, 9.6 percent. The employees who have from one to six short absences per year constitute 78 percent of the total.

However, the proportion of absence-free employees was not always so low in other banks. In one (N = 384) where, typically, there were small branch units of 10–30 employees, the proportion of persons with no short absences over the year was 30.5 percent. The proportion with no absences at all was 27 percent. However, when this sample was separated into males and females, the following distributions were found: 21 percent of 268 females had no absences of any kind, whereas 41 percent of the males (N = 100), who were mainly in managerial grades, had no absences. The distribution patterns are clearly distinct for females and males.

FIGURE 9.1

Distribution of Absences in a General Hospital (N = 619)

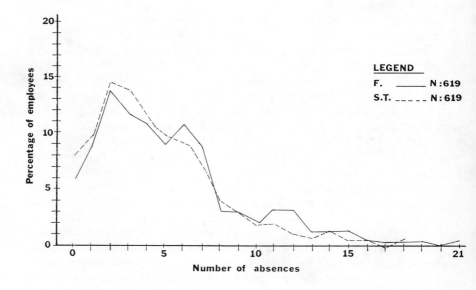

WOMEN'S HIGHER ABSENCE RATES

It has often been observed that in manufacturing occupations women employees have more frequent, short absences than men. We have confirmed this for women employees in clothing manufacture (see Chapter 3) and have demonstrated that women in banks and hospitals have frequent, short absences. Evidently among the reasons behind these frequencies are family responsibilities,

FIGURE 9.2

Distribution of Absences in a Bank (N = 208)

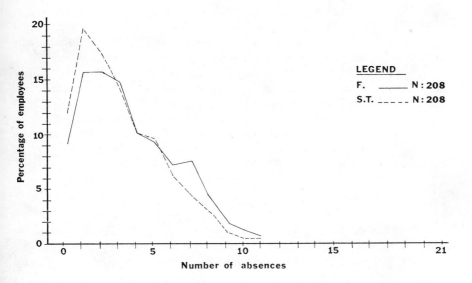

LEGEND

F. _____ N : 208
S.T. _ _ _ _ _ N : 208

children, and home maintenance. The graphs and interviews discussed in Chapter 3 support this conclusion—for example, in the incidence of absences coinciding with school holidays and in the interview discussion of domestic responsibilities. In the literature generally, it has been suggested that these higher trends fluctuate and diminish over the life cycle. It is also not irrelevant that women in manufacturing industries generally hold low-status, lower-paid, and repetitive jobs; possibly women in professional occupations will not have such frequent absences (Thibault 1967). Here again, however, it may be a matter of how much control people in higher-status jobs have over the allocation of their time (for example, by extending a lunch hour or taking an afternoon off without having it recorded as an absence).

In manufacturing industry, previous evidence indicates that women's absences follow a differential pattern. A number of studies show the comparative severity of their absence rates (Schenet 1945; Kerr, Koppelmeier, and Sullivan 1951; Plummer 1960; Kilbridge 1961; Jardillier 1962). However, Simpson (1962), in a study of sickness absence among teachers, found no significant differences between male and female rates where both were in similar jobs. Isambert-Jamati (1962) controlled for occupational levels among female and male employees in eight industrial establishments, and found no absence differences. Some studies draw attention to higher absence rates of maternity age brackets—that is, of women 20–30 years old. According to Hedges (1977), the male/female differences are greatest for the 25–34 age bracket, and absences "for personal reasons" are highest among women in this age group. In an earlier report Hedges (1973) noted that the absence rates of women show life cycle variation, in that the highest between-sex differences in absence rates include 70 percent of the women in the labor force who have children under 18.

Hedges (1973; 1975; 1977) has presented three reports based on U.S. survey data taken from the monthly population survey of households conducted for the U.S. Bureau of Labor Statistics. Although the data tabulations of 1973 in general reveal higher unscheduled absences for women, it is also the case that "Sex differences in absence rates narrow when comparisons are made within a particular occupational group, even though within the group men tend to occupy the better paying jobs" (p. 28).

"CAUSES" AND "CURES" OF ABSENCES

The discussion of "causes" of absenteeism is usually linked to the advocacy of "cures," and both the identification of "causes" and the claims made for "cures" seem to vary with the specializations of different experts. That is, health specialists will advocate health programs; management experts tend to advise creative leadership activities, supervisory controls, or job enrichment; psychologists suggest reinforcement learning and behavior modification methods translated into monetary incentives of various kinds.

There are a number of "remedies" available for absenteeism, such as "chasing down" malingerers, giving closer medical attention to sickness absentees, and trying financial incentives as rewards for a record of uninterrupted attendance. All apparently are effective in the short run (Sanderson 1979 lists a number of these). Evidently, job incentives, supervisory controls, and health programs do contribute to reducing absence levels (Sternhagen 1969), and there are cases reported of each approach working well, but only over the short term.

The multiple causes of absence resist summary in the form of generalizations about strong "cause-effect" linkages. Job dissatisfactions no doubt contribute to absence levels, but the measurable contribution is relatively small (see Chapter 7), as is the proportion of employees in any organization who are completely dissatisfied. Overall or global measures of job satisfaction (that is, where an employee provides a self-assessment of general satisfactions or dissatisfactions with a job) are deficient because they mask the possibility that a satisfied employee may nevertheless find some aspects of the job boring, or at certain periods of the week or month may experience overload.

It is inherently plausible that boredom is one important factor influencing absence rates in some jobs, both white-collar and blue-collar. Some authors have suggested that job redesign or enrichment can reduce absences, although the evidence is by no means as clear-cut as Blackler and Brown (1975) have argued. Job redesign, with its associated reorganization of work teams into small and cohesive units, has been used in assembly-line technologies where jobs traditionally have been fragmented and monotonous and where absenteeism, equally traditionally, is high. Across the 21 organizations where we investigated absenteeism, female assembly-line workers had the highest absences (of all kinds); the lowest short-term levels were found in continuous process industry where men worked in interdependent teams (Chapter 3).

The advocacy of "cures" (and it is assumed by many management writers that a sizable proportion of absences are the result of malingering; see Denett 1978) vacillates between systems of rewards and a variety of "punishments." For example, disciplinary pressures suggested by some authors (such as Gary 1971) take the form of warnings followed by suspensions, and sometimes the use of counseling services in the personnel department. Evidence is not available concerning the long-term effects of disciplinary procedures.

Alternatively, rewards may be allocated to absence-free employees. A variety of methods for reducing absences has been attempted. The U.S. Bureau of National Affairs (1974) states that these methods "include systems for better recording of absences, disciplinary procedures, employee consulting, rewards for good attendance records and special contests or other promotions" (p. 5). In a survey conducted by the bureau, covering 136 organizations of various types, one-quarter of the respondents claimed to use some form of special absence reduction program.

Rewards for good attendance take many forms, including a bonus day off for each six months of absence-free attendance and bonus pay for absence-free quarterly periods. Some firms arrange contests or prize drawings open only to absence-free employees (Nord 1970). Although short-term gains might be expected or claimed, it is not known whether the results are long-lasting.

Psychologists in the behaviorist tradition favor behavior modification or reward techniques (Morgan and Herman 1976), although there is no available validation of such techniques through follow-up studies of the results over the longer term.

In contrast with these approaches to the individual, we would argue that if greater organizational control of absence rates is the objective, the pattern of absences should be discovered (using the sensitive measures discussed in Chapter 3). Second, we would argue that absenteeism is to be understood as a characteristic of the department or organization. The statistical analysis and the explanatory framework will therefore be made at this level, so that they take into account the social pattern of absences.

Some interesting studies have drawn attention to the scope for employee participation in the introduction of financial schemes for good attendance

(Lawler and Hackman 1969; Hackman and Lawler 1971; Schefler, Lawler and Hackman, 1971). Lawler and Hackman demonstrated the effectiveness of participatory schemes as compared with schemes imposed by management. This conclusion is extremely important for any managerial approach to controlling absenteeism. If, as will be suggested below, managements wish to revise the acceptable level of absences within their organizations, then employee participation would appear to be all-important, either through the cooperation of labor unions or through consultative committees set up specifically for this purpose.

AN "ACCEPTABLE" LEVEL OF ABSENTEEISM?

Programs like those just mentioned apparently originate in company policies setting up a level of absences acceptable to management. For example, writers such as Levin (1970) and Clark (1971) argue that once a target is recognized, reviews of employee records should be followed by corrective action to maintain that level. The U.S. Bureau of National Affairs (1974), reporting "on absence reduction programs," cites responses like the following:

> We try to maintain no more than a three per cent to four per cent absence rate and we'll take action if absences exceed this [large manufacturing company].

> Late in 1972 we made a decision that our company was too lax in dealing with absenteeism . . . it was made known that disciplinary action would be taken in the case of excessive absenteeism. Our absenteeism rate was running between five and six per cent at the time. We have reduced our rate to between three and four per cent to date [small manufacturing company].

In a discussion of "avoidable absences" Clark (1971) exhorts managers to "establish standards (maximum acceptable levels of absenteeism/turnover)" (p. 64). Levin (1970) argues for "standards"—"a simple standard might provide for 15 absences per year . . . allowable absenteeism could be permitted to accumulate so that an employee with only eight absences in the first year could be permitted twenty-two in the second . . ." (p. 34). No information is given concerning how these "standards" are determined.

While these exhortations seem to have a rather doubtful basis, the important point to note is that they refer explicitly to a certain level of unscheduled absences as acceptable. We can illustrate this from a study of a Canadian industrial firm (Portis and Bertrand 1978) in which the authors comment that "Foremen were willing to accept some casual absences because of the boring work, so long as it did not become excessive" (p. 33). It is significant in this case that an acceptable level of absences, an absence norm, is recognized openly. Absences up to the acceptable level are even seen as being positive: "Occasional absences were under-

standable and might even lead to better overall effort by individual workers"
(p. 33).

RENEGOTIATING THE NORM

Hypothetically, in a given occupation, if absence levels are largely composed
of longer-term sickness absences, these might be the result of working conditions
and health standards that management cannot (or does not, for whatever reason)
influence. On the other hand, if absence totals are composed of short-term absences, it could justifiably be assumed that there is a de facto management collusion. In such cases, once a statistical analysis had shown that there were high
short-term levels, then, in order to reduce them, it might be argued, management
would have to renegotiate the existing collusive (tacit, informal) agreement concerning existing absence levels.

In their Ontario study Robertson and Humphreys (1978) identified what
amounted to a management tendency to "blame the victim"—that is, to attribute
absences to "personal problems" and "a poor work ethic" among absentee employees. In contrast, it may be useful to think of absence levels as part of an
informal contract between employers and employees. Absences are part of the
package, and renegotiating the package would involve concessions, offers, and
counteroffers between management, unions, and employee representatives.
Thus, reaching agreement on new absence levels could be attempted through
group decision making. This would require beginning with improved measurement techniques, separating sickness and injury (long-term) absences from casual
absences.

Renegotiating absence levels is not any more likely to produce an easy solution than are the "cures" suggested in the literature. There is evidence of a renegotiation taking place unsuccessfully in 1951 between management at the
Ford Motor Company and the United Auto Workers, whereby "the Union
agreed that there would never be more than six per cent of the employees of any
one department absent at any one time. The plan did not work; union officers
could not enforce this scheduled rate" (Gaudet 1963, p. 53). Still, this failure
does not mean that successful negotiations might not be carried through or that
the right package might not be found in other situations.

There seems to be inconsistency between the recognition by some managements that absenteeism constitutes a problem and the reluctance of others to
undertake analysis of absence statistics. Most of the evidence suggests unwilling-
ness and, probably because of it, there is no shortage of exhortatory papers by
management experts advocating that action be taken, for example, through
stricter supervisory and medical surveillance of individual absentees.

In his study of sickness absences Taylor (1974) comments on management
reticence about absence figures in Britain. "Some firms are extremely reticent
about revealing just how much time they do lose due to sickness" (p. 317). The

tendency is also suggested by very low response rates to Labour Department surveys in Nova Scotia (1976) and Ontario (Robertson and Humphreys 1978). In their research on absence rates in Ontario companies, Mikalachki and Chapple (1977) were not allowed to conduct interviews because of "the delicate state of protracted plant negotiations." This is the classic excuse used by managements that simply do not wish to allow research.

In general, the apparent reluctance of managements to study the problem, and to do anything about it, supports the idea of an implicit collusion with existing rates of absenteeism. In white-collar work situations, such as in banks, this might take the form of collusion with occasional short absences; on the other hand, in heavy industry the occasional absences might appear as sickness spells of a week to ten days.

If this hypothetical argument is sound, given rates of absences become, in effect, part of existing (informal) contracts between employers and employees. Thus, any move to reduce the rate would be tantamount to removing an employee benefit—it would alter the balance of social exchange or trade-off between organizations and employees.

To summarize, managements might well encounter union resistance if absence reduction were attempted without the offer of a quid pro quo, possibly the modification of job routines. The important conclusion is therefore that absence levels should be introduced explicitly into the bargaining relationship between employees and managements. It is quite likely that the reported success of "flexitime" (flexible hourly schedules) in lowering absenteeism may be partially explained by the resulting changes in the nature of the job and in work relationships (which are, in effect, given in exchange for improved attendance), in addition to the extra opportunities for leisure that flexible schedules provide.

RENEGOTIATING AND SOCIAL EXCHANGE

For a consensus to be reached between management and unions about absence levels, what might be the nature of the exchange? What might be the quid pro quo for a reduction in absence? Denett (1978) discusses an interesting scheme, called Absence Performance Paid Leave, first introduced at the Citroen Company in 1977. It should be mentioned that such schemes are by no means new. Gaudet's (1963) thorough survey describes several of them. The Citroen scheme provides "an incentive directly geared to the root cause of casual absenteeism, which is that employees, for whatever reason, wish to have more free time. In simple terms, employees are rewarded by a number of paid days leave related to their absence record for the year" (p. 32). The scheme is based on "the principle of increasing leisure time," but ensures a return for the company in improved attendance. The scheme begins with a detailed analysis of absenteeism (the significance of this step cannot be overemphasized). This is followed by a system of maintaining records and monitoring them continuously.

Denett comments: "The disadvantage of the scheme is that setting it up is a complicated process, it is extremely time consuming to administer, and probably of most practical use to companies with excessively high absentee problems." At the same time he gives full importance to the contractual exchange involved in absence rates when he adds: "A scheme of this nature is clearly a matter of negotiation and could have special significance in agreements with a productivity bias, or in a claim for longer holidays or shorter working weeks" (p. 32).

There is some convergence between this practical "how-to-do-it" approach and the analytical categories proposed by Baum and Youngblood (1975), who classify organizational control over absenteeism as deriving from three effective sources: legal controls based on legitimate authority, instrumental controls consisting of valued rewards used as incentives, and intrinsic controls inherent in an attractive job or occupation.

In the case of a renegotiated absence norm, the legal sanctions for new "rules" would be secured in management-union agreements, which could bring into operation the pressures of group commitment in which the force of an additional form of control—social controls—is added to the legal and instrumental ones.

THE COST OF ABSENTEEISM FOR ORGANIZATIONS

Could it be that managements do not see absenteeism as a sufficiently severe cost problem to want to encourage or assist research? Robertson and Humphreys (1978) report in their Ontario study that "The cost of absenteeism ranges from one to three times the hourly rate of the absent workers, depending on whether employees are paid for days absent, whether absent employees are replaced, and who replaces them. Employers reveal that it is common for companies to overstaff by as much as ten percent, particularly in production areas, in order to avoid the disruptive effects of absenteeism" (p. 47). Globerson and Nagarvala (1974) base their estimates of absence cost on a calculation of the size of the standby work force necessary to ensure the minimum number of workers.

Mirvis and Lawler (1977) present an approximate cost analysis of absenteeism in an American bank. Costs are attributed to replacements or extensions of existing staff, and additional fixed costs are incurred from employees' fringe benefits, supervisors' time spent in finding a replacement, and "the under-absorbed overhead rate" (including the expense of lights and rent). The authors caution that the cost of absenteeism will vary widely between organizations, and that probably they are relatively low in banks because the teller's job does not require heavy investment in training and recruitment.

Despite the obvious difficulties in making general estimates, there is widespread agreement that absences constitute a large cost item. A report from the U.S. Department of Labor (1972) mentions that some employers, in estimating absence cost, equate every 1 percent of absence to 1 percent of lost profits. An earlier report (U.S. Department of Labor 1951) referred to an estimate in the automobile industry "that each per cent of absenteeism in the plants reduced production about 2.5 per cent"—an estimate that produces a heavy cost figure. In other situations the calculation of cost gives impressive figures even if based only on the loss in salary payments to absent employees (see Clark 1971). Nord (1970) has discussed the cost to a U.S. school system of providing substitute teachers, again a substantial item.

There is no doubting the evidence about absenteeism cost; it is overwhelmingly clear that managements face a very large cost item, irrespective of whether we examine the national cost estimates or the organizational estimates. Gaudet (1963) attempted a detailed breakdown of absence costs; as with absence statistics of any kind, the number of industries and companies able to provide any sort of cost analysis was extremely small. An important factor noted by Gaudet, and that currently shows little sign of changing, was "the apparent lack of management interest in labour wastage . . . a constant source of amazement to the investigators" (p. 53). Here again we return to the likelihood of management collusion with prevailing absence rates, and to the notion that absenteeism is part of an informal contract.

One last (optimistic) indication lies in the possibility of applying computer methods to the analysis of absences (Scherba and Smith 1973; Butler and Hay 1977). Computerization of absence statistics may be a positive development, however, only with full awareness of different measurement procedures, such as we have described.

10

CONCLUSIONS

The correlational results (see Chapter 7) gave slight support to the notion of inverse relationships between job satisfactions and absence rates, and suggested that job satisfactions are among many influences on these decisions to be absent or that questionnaires provide a static measure, only superficially touching a set of deeper continuous relationships.

Thus, the failure to show stronger associations might be the result of the JSQ's being too superficial a test of intentions operative in decisions to be absent from work. The original instrument was applied in correlational studies with absence totals by Smith, Kendall, and Hulin (1969). Coefficients of the order of 0.3 were obtained (which did not appreciably account for common variance between the two variables of more than some 13 percent). Most similar studies have reported coefficients at even lower levels.

There might also be failings in the methods of measuring absence behavior. This is less likely to be the case because, by using measures such as the short-term index, we aimed to isolate the part of absence behavior resulting from deliberate decisions to stay away from work. At the same time, as was discussed in Chapter 4, even the short-term measures are not uncontaminated by sickness absences.

Given that more precise distinctions are not possible, but that the frequency and short-term indices are both sensitive indicators, we are left with the question of what degree of correlation we should expect between them and measures of job satisfactions. The answer is a very low degree indeed.

From the only other existing study on a similar scale, in which data on 2,209 individuals were analyzed (Gadourek 1965), we can confirm that correlations are extremely low. Gadourek makes this comment, referring to his correlation matrix:

These low values are striking, indeed; though we fixed the level of significance at such a low value of the coefficient as 0.05, there are but

few predictor variables that pass this test and are significantly associated with the main dependent variables . . . [the table] in fact, shows
how difficult it is to find *any* meaningful correlations, even those as
are expected on theoretical grounds. (p. 120)

Correlational studies of absence behavior and attitudes fail to provide evidence of associations of a high order, possibly because of faults in the measuring techniques or because the correlational matrix provides a static represen-
tation of dynamic situations. Added to these possibilities are the obvious deficiencies of job satisfaction questionnaires that in general evade issues of union
membership and affiliations to groups.

The correlational analysis that we undertook—between three absence measures and scores on a job satisfaction questionnaire—resulted in the disappointing
coefficients that are usual in this kind of study. Nevertheless, our correlations of
absence measures with age brackets of employees generally confirmed relationships in the expected direction between (lower) short-term rates and (higher) age
levels. The correlational analysis of Chapter 5 was useful in pointing to some
association between short-term absences and labor turnover and, more especially, in giving confirmation to the covariation of short-term absences (as a
measure of "voluntary" absence) with the tendency for absences to occur sys-
tematically on certain days (the Worst Day Index). In the latter case, the correlations were based on observations over time periods, or repeated measures, in
contrast to the one-off test of job satisfactions.

Moreover, the use of a socially based theory (as discussed in Chapter 5) produced data collection methods quite different from the conventional approach
to job satisfactions. These alternative methods were completely successful in
demonstrating organizational and occupational patterns that were distinctive.
They enabled us to assume the operation of employees' shared expectations
about appropriate levels of absences, evolving in the particular conditions of
each occupational category. The interview material gave insights into employees'
thinking about their absences from work, suggesting that these absences were
purposive and that they gave access to social activities, although a relatively
small but persistent proportion clearly provided relief from episodic job pressures.

We have criticized approaches to absenteeism that are tied to individual
psychology and to theories of individual motivation. We have argued for an
approach to absenteeism as a widespread form of social behavior, and we have
suggested that absences be understood as part of a social exchange between
employees and managements. Taking this theoretical position means that we
have used sources of data in addition to the attitude-questionnaire analysis typical of absence studies. We have summarized data by organizational and by occupational categories in the yearly histograms and trends; we have sought information by interviewing people in various organizations on the topic of absence
from work.

In Chapter 2 we drew attention to a distinction that should be made between collecting information from individuals about their behavior and explain-

ing that behavior in an individual frame of reference. The first, as part of a research procedure with data collection from individuals leading to explanations in terms of social behavior, is an appropriate sequence. The second involves a basic error in theorizing. While it may be assumed, as a philosophical position, that individuals are acting freely, we should also assume that they will act in relation to existing rules and social conditions. Thus, absence behavior can be adequately understood only as a form of social behavior in a given context. Our argument, supported by the empirical results of this study, is that it would be erroneous to try to make a conceptual separation of individuals from their memberships in actual occupational groups.

The organizational and occupational patterns that have been demonstrated in our results show that absences are far from being a matter of "individual responses" in the abstract. It follows (because absence is social behavior) that any attempt at control must be exercised by or through occupational and work groups. In view of the data we have presented on absence distributions, it would be useless to look for long-term reductions in absenteeism rates by "chasing down" individual malingerers. It would be more sensible to discover the pattern of absences pertaining to departments and organizations, thus identifying the social pattern of absences in these social entities. This can be done if there are a number of sensitive absence measures so that the pattern will emerge clearly in the ways we have demonstrated in earlier chapters. Lower absence levels might possibly be negotiated at the group level, rather than as management action taken against individuals.

Attempts to control absences imposed by management may well be resisted by an occupational group. If management considers absenteeism to be too high, a more positive strategy would be to approach representatives of the group and agree with them on an appropriate level. In this case bargaining between management and employee representatives would be involved, and it might be necessary to offer a quid pro quo—that is, concessions of some kind in exchange for the desired reduction in absences. As was seen in Chapter 9, at least one such attempt is recorded as having failed, and in the end we have to admit that this solution, although it is theoretically sound and practical, may depend on some of the following questions: How do we know that management bargaining procedures have been adequate? How favorable is the climate [the previous history] in a particular context of industrial relations or management-union relationships? How adequately is the occupational group represented by union officials? Are informal representatives more effective in influencing group members? With so many questions we can only offer cautious advocacy that this type of solution might be effective, but from the social nature of the absence phenomena that we have documented in this book, it seems to be sound advice.

Another possibility would involve reconsidering the artifactual nature of fixed working hours and the practicality of flexible schedules.

Cohen and Gadon (1978) have discussed the broad scope of innovative work schedules, especially flexible hourly arrangements, which they consider to be appropriate for segments of the work force who are "younger, older and female." There are also those who want "to trade income for time off." Cohen and Gadon give the examples of payment plans where reductions in income are taken in exchange for days off (a 5 percent reduction for 10.5 days off, a 10 percent reduction for 21 days off). There are a number of management papers advocating new work schedules as an answer to unemployment. Best and Stern (1977) estimated a reduction in U.S. unemployment of 1 percent if half the labor force were to exchange 2 percent of their income for one additional paid week of vacation.

Cohen and Gadon discuss flexible working hours as "essentially a work schedule that gives employees daily choice in the timing between work and non-work activities" (1978, p. 34). It involves the notion of a band width of 12-16 hours per day divided into core time and flexible time. Core time (for example, 9 A.M.-11 A.M., 1 P.M.-3 P.M.) represents those hours when every employee has to be at work; flexible time represents the hours when employees can decide for themselves when to come or go (for example, 6:30 A.M.-9 A.M., 11 A.M.-1 P.M., 3 P.M.-5:30 P.M.). There may be a carry-forward of debit (due hours not worked) or credit (hours worked in excess). There are difficulties with such schemes because of overtime regulations. Cohen and Gadon also argue for a number of other arrangements, such as the "variable hours" scheme in which people work according to the demands of the job (farmers and academics can be said to be on variable hours).

Among the possible disadvantages of flexible working schedules are the additional planning and analysis required of managements, problems of keeping cumulative records of hours worked, coverage of "unpopular" days or hours, and higher overheads. On the other hand, flexible hours would be particularly to the advantage of working mothers and, as Cohen and Gadon mention, "single individuals who lead an active night life"(!)

Unfortunately, current discussions of flexible working hours vacillate between general discussion of "the individual's" preferences and very broad classifications such as "elderly," "young," and "preretirement" categories. However, it seems (logically) that, in many contexts, flexible schedules could remove absenteeism as prevalent social behavior.

We have mentioned flexible hours as a likely counter to absenteeism problems at a practical level. We believe that the research results must necessarily be used in dealing with practical problems, as Broadbent (1980) advocates. There is no doubt that it is very difficult to combine research with practical objectives, certainly in any immediate and direct way. We have sought in this book to present research information and to pose questions about absenteeism in different forms than hitherto. We have argued that absenteeism is to be analyzed, explained, and understood at a social level, and at the same time we have demonstrated the use of an array of measures that offer alternatives to the disappointing correlational studies of attitudes.

APPENDIX A:
THE JOB SATISFACTION
QUESTIONNAIRE

The questionnaire that we devised to measure job satisfactions was intended to conform to three main criteria. First, it was to be of established validity and reliability. Second, it would be suitable for employee samples of varying educational level. Third, it was to provide an assessment of attitudes toward separate aspects of the work situation in addition to a measure of "global" job satisfaction.

The Job Description Index (JDI) developed by a team at Cornell University (Smith, Kendall, and Hulin 1969) met these requirements in the following ways. It had been thoroughly tested; details of its construction, validation, and norms are available. The testing procedures covered a variety of occupations. The questionnaire was easy to use and to score, comprising a series of adjective checklists relating to five job areas: work itself, pay, promotion opportunities, supervision, and people (co-workers). Aggregate overall satisfaction scores could be derived from the combined subscale scores. These job areas are well validated as independent dimensions of job satisfactions (Hinrichs 1968).

In pilot trials, modifications were made to the JDI that eventually produced the Job Satisfaction Questionnaire (JSQ). For instance, we removed items that required respondents to perform difficult double negations (such as "no privacy" in the people scale). Items were also removed or replaced because their descriptive emphasis (as opposed to evaluative emphasis) might reflect objective differences in technology and job setting rather than employees' attitudes to them (for example, the item "hot" on the work scale). Items were also removed that might be unacceptable in some work situations, in particular those critical of supervision and co-workers. The scales were also shortened by removing redundant items.

These changes resulted in the 50-item questionnaire that covered the same five job areas as the original JDI. Items deleted from the JDI were the following:

Work scale: fascinating, good, respectable, hot, tiresome, healthful, on your feet, gives sense of accomplishment

Pay scale: bad, underpaid

Promotion scale: unfair promotion policy, good opportunity for advancement, opportunities somewhat limited, good chance for promotion, fairly good chance for promotions, promotion on ability (modified)

Supervision scale: tactful, annoying, bad, up-to-date, doesn't supervise enough, lazy, quick tempered, tells me where I stand

People scale: stupid, fast, easy to make enemies, smart, unpleasant, no privacy, active, hard to meet.

Some minor changes were made in the introductory wording of the questionnaire as a result of comments from respondents and management. The new items and their item-whole (point-biserial) correlations are shown below:

Work scale: responsible (.38); tiring (.41); healthy (.39)
Promotion scale: fair (.39); based mainly on ability (.42); reasonable opportunities (.44); the promotion opportunities I deserve (.42)
Supervision scale: supervises too much (.46); decisive (.42).

It is interesting that many of the changes made were remarkably similar to those made independently by Cross (1973) in his extensively validated version of the instrument: the Worker Opinion Survey.

One means of maintaining a running check on the scales is the incorporation of overall satisfaction bipolar rating scales for each of the job areas, a procedure adopted by Warr and Routledge (1969) in their managerial version of the JDI. Scales similar to these were appended to each of the subscales in the JSQ, so that their concurrent validity could be assessed against these more simple global ratings.

Respondents were asked to identify themselves on the first page of the questionnaire by giving their clock number, in the interest of the individual correlations of absence and attitude data. They were also asked to state their age, length of service, and marital status, thus permitting our subsequent correlations of personal characteristics and absence rates. To reduce the likelihood of evoking the mistrust of respondents, in all organizations the first period of fieldwork was devoted to extensive information and explanatory discussions with managers, trade union officials, and employees.

APPENDIX B:
RESULTS: JOB SATISFACTION
QUESTIONNAIRE PROFILES

In this appendix we will compare the Job Satisfaction Questionnaire (JSQ) with the Cornell Job Description Index (JDI) in terms of the sample distribution of scores on each of the five job satisfaction areas. We will test concurrent validity of the subscales with Likert-type scales; it will be shown that these co-efficients and comparable Cornell data were of similar magnitude. Also discussed in this appendix are importance rankings of the five subscales (work, pay, promotion, supervision, people). Last, we examine subscale interrelationships.

In order to facilitate evaluation of the revised scales' validity, the sample distributions (four samples for each of the four blue-collar industries) are summarized, scale by scale, in Tables B.2 to B.6, and the Cornell standardization data are summarized in Table B.1. This table shows the population percentile values of scores at the midpoints of the ranges for each scale and, in parentheses, the skew this represents.

TABLE B.1

Cornell JDI Norms: Scale Midpoint Percentile
Values and Direction of Skew
(N = approx. 1,950 males; 635 females)

JDI Scale	Males	Females
Work	47.5 (nil)	50.0 (nil)
Pay	66.7 (pos.)	75.0 (pos.)
Promotion	81.0 (pos.)	89.6 (pos.)
Supervision	30.0 (neg.)	30.0 (neg.)
People	22.5 (neg.)	27.5 (neg.)

Source: Derived from Smith, Kendall, and Hulin 1969, p. 106.

Comparing the skew in this table with our own data reveals that there is a fairly close correspondence between them. Insofar as similarity of response distributions indicates concurrent validity, the JSQ appears to perform very satisfactorily. The most "deviant" of the revised scales is the work scale, which has a tendency toward positive skew in the JSQ (more people expressing dis-

TABLE B.2

Descriptive Profiles of the JSQ Distributions for Sixteen Samples and Four Group Totals: Work Scale

Group Code	1			2			3			4			Total		
	Median	Kurtosis*	Skew	Median	Kurtosis	Skew	Median	Kurtosis	Skew	Median	Kurtosis	Skew	Median	Kurtosis	Skew
A	16.0	40%	pos.	14.0	35%	pos.	15.9	35%	pos.	15.1	40%	pos.	15.3	40%	pos.
B	15.0	35%	pos.	15.2	40%	pos.	18.1	35%	nil	20.0	35%	nil (bimodal)	15.3	30%	pos.
C	13.3	35%	pos.	15.0	30%	pos.	18.3	35%	nil	21.2	35%	neg.	17.9	30%	pos.
D	20.0	30%	nil	15.4	40%	pos.	18.8	30%	nil	20.9	30%	nil	19.1	30%	nil

Range = 0–39; midpoint = 19.5.

*The amount of kurtosis is described by the percentage of the sample with scores in the modal class interval, there being five class intervals to the range of each scale. The percentages are rounded to the nearest 5 percent, and a score of 30 percent or less is broadly indicative of platykursis; 45 percent and more, of leptokursis; and 35–40 percent, of a more normal shape.

TABLE B.3

Descriptive Profiles of the JSQ Distributions for Sixteen Samples and Four Group Totals: Pay Scale

Group Code	Sample Code														Total		
	1			2			3			4							
	Median	Kurtosis*	Skew	Median	Kurtosis	Skew	Median	Kurtosis	Skew	Median	Kurtosis	Skew			Median	Kurtosis	Skew
A	6.0	40%	strong pos.	8.6	40%	strong pos.	6.2	35%	strong pos.	10.2	30%	pos.			7.1	50%	strong pos.
B	6.9	35%	pos.	3.4	55%	strong pos.	3.5	50%	strong pos.	6.2	40%	strong pos.			6.1	40%	strong pos.
C	8.0	30%	strong pos. (bimodal)	8.4	30%	strong pos. (bimodal)	6.2	30%	strong pos.	8.9	30%	nil			7.8	30%	strong pos.
D	5.5	45%	strong pos.	4.2	55%	strong pos.	3.8	55%	strong pos.	6.2	40%	strong pos.			5.5	50%	strong pos.

Range = 0–21; midpoint = 10.5.

*The amount of kurtosis is described by the percentage of the sample with scores in the modal class interval, there being five class intervals to the range of each scale. The percentages are rounded to the nearest 5 percent, and a score of 30 percent or less is broadly indicative of platykursis; 45 percent and more, of leptokursis; and 35–40 percent, of a more normal shape.

TABLE B.4

Descriptive Profiles of the JSQ Distributions for
Sixteen Samples and Four Group Totals: Promotion Scale

Group Code	Sample Code														Total		
	1			2			3			4							
	Median	Kurtosis*	Skew	Median	Kurtosis	Skew	Median	Kurtosis	Skew	Median	Kurtosis	Skew		Median	Kurtosis	Skew
A	6.1	40%	strong pos.	5.7	45%	strong pos.	6.4	45%	strong pos.	8.1	30%	strong pos.		6.4	35%	strong pos.
B	6.3	40%	strong pos.	7.5	40%	strong pos.	4.2	55%	strong pos.	5.8	40%	strong pos.		6.2	40%	strong pos.
C	3.3	60%	strong pos.	4.2	50%	strong pos.	6.3	35%	strong pos.	10.1	20%	nil		6.0	40%	strong pos.
D	5.7	45%	strong pos.	5.6	45%	strong pos.	4.5	50%	strong pos.	7.7	30%	strong pos.		5.8	40%	strong pos.

Range = 0–24; midpoint = 12.0.

*The amount of kurtosis is described by the percentage of the sample with scores in the modal class interval, there being five class intervals to the range of each scale. The percentages are rounded to the nearest 5 percent, and a score of 30 percent or less is broadly indicative of platykursis; 45 percent and more, of leptokursis; and 35–40 percent, of a more normal shape.

TABLE B.5

Descriptive Profiles of the JSQ Distribution for
Sixteen Samples and Four Group Totals: Supervision Scale

Group Code	1 Median	Kurtosis*	Skew	2 Median	Kurtosis	Skew	3 Median	Kurtosis	Skew	4 Median	Kurtosis	Skew	Total Median	Kurtosis	Skew
A	27.6	40%	strong neg.	26.0	40%	strong neg.	25.7	35%	strong neg.	20.6	30%	neg.	25.3	35%	strong neg.
B	22.5	30%	neg.	24.8	30%	strong neg.	17.8	25%	nil	18.5	25%	nil	21.4	25%	neg.
C	19.3	35%	nil	23.3	35%	strong neg. (trimodal)	27.1	45%	strong neg.	28.8	45%	strong neg.	25.0	35%	strong neg.
D	13.5	30%	pos.	15.3	25%	nil	15.2	30%	pos.	17.8	25%	pos. (bimodal)	15.2	25%	pos.

Range = 0–36; midpoint = 18.0.

*The amount of kurtosis is described by the percentage of the sample with scores in the modal class interval, there being five class intervals to the range of each scale. The percentages are rounded to the nearest 5 percent, and a score of 30 percent or less is broadly indicative of platykursis; 45 percent and more, of leptokursis; and 35–40 percent, of a more normal shape.

TABLE B.6

Descriptive Profiles of the JSQ Distributions for Sixteen Samples and Four Group Totals: People Scale

Group	Sample Code												Total		
	1			2			3			4					
Code	Median	Kurtosis*	Skew	Median	Kurtosis	Skew	Median	Kurtosis	Skew	Median	Kurtosis	Skew	Median	Kurtosis	Skew
A	22.6	40%	strong neg.	22.9	40%	strong neg.	24.5	50%	strong neg.	21.4	40%	strong neg.	22.6	40%	strong neg.
B	23.0	45%	strong neg.	21.8	40%	neg.	18.8	30%	neg.	19.0	40%	neg.	21.2	35%	strong neg.
C	23.6	35%	strong neg.	21.6	30%	neg.	26.7	55%	strong neg.	23.5	35%	strong neg.	23.7	40%	strong neg.
D	20.6	35%	neg.	15.4	30%	nil	15.5	30%	nil (bimodal)	12.3	25%	pos.	16.4	25%	neg.

Range = 0–30; midpoint = 15.0.

*The amount of kurtosis is described by the percentage of the sample with scores in the modal class inteval, there being five class intervals to the range of each scale. The percentages are rounded to the nearest 5 percent, and a score of 30 percent or less is broadly indicative of platykursis; 45 percent and more, of leptokursis; and 35–40 percent, of a more normal shape.

satisfaction than in the Cornell studies). (See Table B.2.) This deviation is not sufficiently marked to cast doubt on the scale's validity: what skew there is in other Cornell samples is in the same direction. The deviation possibly reflects greater job dissatisfaction of British compared with American workers. However, the difference is marginal; in groups A to C people are rather evenly divided into satisfied and dissatisfied categories on this scale. As in all other tables, Group A is clothing manufacture; Group B, foundries; Group C, automated process; and Group D, public transport.

On the pay scale (Table B.3) dissatisfaction is prevalent in all but one of our samples—that is, there is a strongly positive skew in all but one instance (C4). An almost identical pattern appears on the promotion scale (Table B.4), with C4 again the sole exception to the recurring positive skew. As was the case in the Cornell data, the skew is here more pronounced for the promotion than for the pay scale. An opposite trend appears on the supervision (Table B.5) and people (Table B.6) scales, where the negative skew shows that only a small minority in most samples are dissatisfied. The Cornell workers also found less dissatisfaction with people than with supervision. This is not the case for the D Group samples (public transport), which include far larger proportions of workers expressing dissatisfaction with people. This was an artifact of the somewhat vague term "people": in bus companies "people on your present job" was understood to include the traveling public, about whom busmen's feelings were not so positive as they were about colleagues. Thus, the Cornell researchers' interchangeable use of "people" and "co-workers" is clearly invalid when the job content requires social interaction with people other than fellow employees.

INTERSAMPLE DIFFERENCES AND IMPORTANCE RANKINGS

Table B.7 tabulates the number of statistically significant differences between the samples in each of the organizations on all five subscales.

TABLE B.7

Number of Significant Intersample Differences on the Five JSQ Scales

Scale	A Group	B Group	C Group	D Group	Between All Groups
Work	2	0	5	1	5
Pay	3	2	1	0	4
Promotion	4	1	4	1	2
Supervision	5	2	3	1	5
People	3	0	2	2	5

One feature is immediately apparent: the number of differences within groups (out of a possible six significant differences) is nonrandomly distributed across scales and groups. It seems that the B and D group samples are far more homogeneous in their job satisfaction profile than are the samples of the other two groups, among which there are more frequent significant differences. Moreover, these differences emerge most often on the work, promotion, and supervision scales, while the sample profiles are more similar on the pay and people scales. It may be suggested tentatively that this is evidence of greater similarity on the objective levels of pay and type of social environment within organizational categories than there is between job content, promotion opportunities, and supervisory practices.

On the work scale (see Table B.2) it seems that the busmen (D) derive most enjoyment from their jobs, followed by the automated process operators (C), while the sewing machine operators (A) and foundry workers (B) tend to be less satisfied. Although a majority of the respondents in all groups are dissatisfied with pay, this finding is least marked among the relatively highly paid automated process operators (Table B.3). Female sewing machine operators are highly satisfied with supervision (Table B.5), and indicate satisfaction with the way supervisors are chosen from among them.

The high satisfaction of the sewing machine operators is probably a product of the supportive, and even "maternal," role of supervisors in clothing factories. In contrast, for automated process operators (see Table B.5), it is probably an effect of freedom from close supervision and their considerable job autonomy. Only in transport companies are a majority of respondents dissatisfied with supervision. The explanation for this is to be found in the large differences in the supervisory function in public transport compared with manufacturing industry. In the former, supervision follows quasi-militaristic lines, and the role of inspector is primarily rule-enforcing, rather than a technical or socially supportive one. The atypical scores for Group D on the people scale have already been discussed, and although other groups are not sharply differentiated on this scale, social bonds appear to be strongest among the automated process operators and sewing machine operators.

A further addition to the questionnaire was a single item asking respondents to rank the five job satisfaction areas in order of subjective importance (see also Mikes and Hulin 1968; Smith, Kendall, and Hulin 1969; Blood 1971). In the importance rankings (Table B.8) the degree of intersample unanimity is remarkably high. Pay is almost universally accorded the highest ranking, work is the second most favored job area, followed by people, while promotion and supervision are rated as least important. The only intergroup difference worthy of note is in the rank ordering of the latter two job satisfaction areas. The lowest ranking of supervision in Groups C and D may be a product of the greater remoteness of supervision in these two industries. However, differences are too slight to sustain other than the most tentative of interpretations. General dissatisfaction with pay across all samples is also worth noting, as well as its high ranking in terms of importance.

TABLE B.8

Mean Importance Rankings of the Five Job Satisfaction Areas

Sample	Work	Pay	Promotion	Supervision	People
A1	2.36	1.32	4.46	3.58	3.29
A2	2.38	1.56	4.47	3.47	3.03
A3	2.38	1.45	4.55	3.76	2.86
A4	2.06	1.76	4.54	3.83	2.80
Group A Total	2.29	1.50	4.50	3.67	3.02
B1	2.71	1.34	3.77	3.86	3.32
B2	2.67	1.79	3.88	3.72	2.95
B3	2.37	1.77	3.70	3.85	3.30
B4	2.55	1.50	4.50	3.60	2.85
Group B Total	2.60	1.57	3.84	3.80	3.18
C1	2.11	1.29	4.20	4.34	3.06
C2	2.63	1.73	2.82	4.13	3.68
C3	2.13	1.72	3.32	4.59	3.24
C4	2.31	1.60	3.41	4.34	3.34
Group C Total	2.27	1.59	3.46	4.37	3.31
D1	2.37	1.57	3.94	4.13	3.00
D2	2.44	1.70	3.65	3.98	3.27
D3	2.29	1.67	3.71	4.00	3.32
D4	2.25	1.45	3.41	4.33	3.59
Group D Total	2.34	1.59	3.69	4.12	3.28
Grand Total	2.36	1.55	3.94	3.96	3.18

However, the ranking procedure used here has many drawbacks, and its validity as a means of assessing the motivational significance of various satisfactions and dissatisfactions is questionable. It is an ipsative technique; items can be ranked higher only at the expense of others; it is superficial in the sense that it provides only an abstract word list to represent factors that in reality interact with each other in the dynamics of work situations. Last, that pay is given greatest importance is probably a relatively trivial discovery. Conventionally, this could be expected to be the case for most industrial occupations; it is also a sensible message for employees to convey to managements (since they knew that the questionnaire results would be reported to the latter). Avoiding these disadvantages is achieved only through interview methods (see Chadwick-Jones 1969; Mobley and Locke 1970).

LIKERT-TYPE SCALES

The inclusion in the questionnaire of simple nine-point rating scales in addition to the checklist items in each of the JSQ areas was intended to achieve a concurrent check. Correlations between the JSQ scores and these ratings cannot strictly be interpreted as dependable validity coefficients because the two measurement methods are conceptually distinct. For example, the JSQ has descriptive items in addition to the purely evaluative, while the Likert-type scales require respondents to make a simple evaluation of various aspects of their jobs. Nevertheless, correlations between the two types of scale provided evidence of the degree to which they might be conceptually divergent. Since the Likert-type measures are operatively identical, differences between their correlations with the JSQ scales may be safely attributed to variation in the performance of the latter; major fluctuations in their interrelationships might be taken as probably indicative of weaknesses in the JSQ.

Table B.9 tabulates the coefficients for each of the five scale areas across all samples.

The results of the present study do not differ much from those of the Cornell workers in the overall predictability of one type of measure from the other—correlations are of roughly the same order of magnitude for samples of similar size. There are, however, differences in the relative strengths and weaknesses of individual scales. For example, the promotion scale appears to be more erratic than others. It is probably the least relevant to blue-collar samples, since their opportunities for advancement are generally limited. However, the items of this scale make it possible to capture worker attitudes not purely restricted to promotion opportunities. Responses to certain promotion items may reflect employee attitudes to management and the organization in general (for instance, items asking if the respondent sees the system as "fair" or the job as a "dead-end" one). In fact, there is probably a good case to be made for measuring attitudes in the related areas of "management" and "organization" for blue-

TABLE B.9

Correlations Between JSQ and Likert-Type Scales

Sample	N	Work	Pay	Prom.	Supe.	People
A1	146	.36	.50	.48	.59	.55
A2	66	.50	.66	.42	.68	.56
A3	96	.48	.54	.58	.61	.51
A4	103	.55	.68	.50	.80	.65
B1	102	.41	.47	.54	.69	.62
B2	58	.48	.60	.73	.64	.59
B3	62	.39	.44	.49	.57	.59
B4	20	.25	.40	.31	.64	.48
C1	73	.53	.55	.43	.70	.70
C2	61	.57	.72	.72	.78	.75
C3	85	.57	.34	.61	.80	.50
C4	80	.52	.54	.73	.76	.76
D1	76	.51	.34	.62	.67	.53
D2	63	.53	.37	.65	.67	.49
D3	58	.64	.59	.43	.43	.69
D4	73	.64	.43	.65	.70	.63
Gp. A	411	.47	.62	.47	.69	.56
Gp. B	242	.40	.52	.56	.66	.60
Gp. C	299	.54	.56	.67	.75	.69
Gp. D	270	.60	.43	.59	.65	.59
Total	1,222	.51	.56	.58	.71	.63

TABLE B.10

Cornell JDI "Faces" Correlation Coefficients
(N = 80 blue-collar males)

Scale	r
Work	.75
Pay	.72
Promotion	.64
Supervision	.78
People	.57

Source: Derived from Smith, Kendall, and Hulin (1969, p. 76).

collar-samples, a case that has been both recognized and demonstrated elsewhere (Cross 1973; Hinrichs 1968).

Table B.10 shows the correlations obtained by the Cornell authors of the original JDI with a similar overall measure of job satisfaction (the "Faces" scale). The "Faces" measure consisted of a six-point response scale depicted in the form of six cartoon faces expressing emotions from extreme liking to disliking (see Smith, Kendall, and Hulin 1969, p. 49); it is analogous to the Likert-type scales used here, insofar as it taps the purely evaluative dimension of job satisfaction.

CORRELATIONS BETWEEN SUBSCALES

Smith, Kendall, and Hulin (1969, pp. 77-78) found statistically significant intercorrelations for all combinations of subscales, and argued that their results indicated a job satisfaction structure consisting of a general satisfaction factor and partly overlapping specific job area satisfactions (those of the five subscales). The results of the present study are broadly similar, though the overlap of scales is rather less pronounced and less uniform between different pairs. These results are summarized in Table B.11.

The uneven overlap of scales shown in this table is the principal feature of interest in these results. The scale most contiguous with others, and thus following the reasoning of the Cornell authors, the most general facet of job satisfaction, is the work scale. The people and pay scales, on the other hand, behave more independently than others.

The results show a tendency for the supervision and people scales to intercorrelate strongly, and for the pay and promotion scales to do likewise; at the same time these two pairings are relatively independent. This suggests that the Cornell analysis, according equal, semi-independent status to subscales, may not always be the most applicable.

An alternative explanation would assume the existence of a general factor, predominantly weighted by attitudes toward the work itself, and two overlapping, more specific areas of social satisfaction (comprising attitudes toward supervision and co-workers) and reward satisfaction (comprising attitudes toward pay and promotion). However, to confirm this hypothesis would require, ideally, an analysis of a large pool of items covering a wider content than the JDI or JSQ.

A final feature of interest in these results, in Table B.11, is the fact that there is a stronger and more uniform overlap between the Likert-type scales than there is between the JSQ scales. This is not an unexpected finding, in view of the greater objective similarity in the format and wording of the five Likert-type scales (the similarity of the response format in the latter is more likely to evoke a uniform response set than are the adjective checklist-type JSQ scales). Moreover, while all the Likert-type scales are ostensibly evaluative, and not descrip-

TABLE B.11

Job Satisfaction Subscale Interrelationships

JSQ Scales						Likert-Type Scales				

JSQ	work	pay	prom.	supe.		Likert	work	pay	prom.	supe.
Pay	4					Pay	4			
Prom.	3	3				Prom.	3	4		
Supe.	3	1	3			Supe.	3	2	4	
People	2	1	1	4	Group A*	People	3	1	2	4
Pay	2					Pay	2			
Prom.	3	2				Prom.	2	2		
Supe.	3	1	2			Supe.	2	2	2	
People	3	0	2	2	Group B*	People	1	2	1	2
Pay	2					Pay	4			
Prom.	3	4				Prom.	4	4		
Supe.	2	2	3			Supe.	4	3	4	
People	3	1	1	3	Group C*	People	3	3	3	4
Pay	3					Pay	4			
Prom.	4	3				Prom.	4	2		
Supe.	4	2	4			Supe.	4	4	4	
People	4	1	0	2	Group D*	People	3	2	3	3

JSQ	work	pay	prom.	supe.		Likert	work	pay	prom.	supe.
Pay	11					Pay	14			
Prom.	13	12				Prom.	13	12		
Supe.	12	6	12			Supe.	13	11	14	
People	12	3	4	11	Total**	People	10	8	9	13
Pay	4					Pay	4			
Prom.	4	4				Prom.	4	4		
Supe.	4	3	4			Supe.	4	4	4	
People	4	1	2	4	All Groups*	People	4	4	3	4

*Cell totals = the number of samples, of a possible maximum of four, for which the intercorrelation of two subscales is significant at or beyond the 5 percent confidence limit.

**As cell totals, but out of possible maximum of 16 significant intercorrelations.

tive, the JSQ scales are composed of both types of item; the divergence of these dimensions in attitude measurement has been demonstrated by Payne, Fineman, and Wall (1975).

APPENDIX C:
INTERCORRELATIONS
BETWEEN ABSENCE MEASURES

TABLE C.1

Intercorrelations Between Absence Measures:
Individual Yearly Rates

Firm	N	TL/F	TL/ST	F/ST
A1	146	.418***	.104	.867***
A2	66	.765***	.588***	.952***
A3	96	.560***	.378***	.964***
A4	103	.492***	.357***	.966***
B1	102	.532***	.329***	.920***
B2	58	.430***	.305*	.973***
B3	62	.462***	.111	.889***
B4	20	.472*	.079	.865***
C1	73	.680***	.410***	.887***
C2	61	.606***	.392***	.918***
C3	85	.463***	.172	.820***
C4	80	.726***	.282*	.744***
D1	76	.172	.059	.969***
D2	63	.306*	.135	.963***
D3	58	.206	.035	.954***
D4	73	.331**	.216	.968***
E1	185	.602***	.377***	.929***
E2	386	.579***	.344***	.931***
E3	72	.555***	.431***	.978***
F1	619	.748***	.520***	.917***
F2	322	.628***	.422***	.941***

*p < .05.
**p < .01.
***p < .001.

BIBLIOGRAPHY

Acton Society Trust (1953). Size and Morale. 2 vols. London.

Adams, J. S. (1965). Inequity in social exchange. Advances in Experimental Social Psychology, 2, 267-299.

Argyle, M., G. Gardner, and F. Cioffi (1958). Supervisory methods related to productivity, absenteeism, and labour turnover. Human Relations, 11, 32-40.

Ås, D. (1962). Absenteeism—a social fact in need of a theory. Acta Sociologica, 6, 278-285.

Baum, J. F., and S. A. Youngblood (1975). Impact of an organizational control policy on absenteeism, performance and satisfaction. Journal of Applied Psychology, 60, 688-694.

Baumgartel, H., and R. Sobol (1959). Background and organisational factors in absenteeism. Personnel Psychology, 12, 432-443.

Behrend, H. (1951). Absence under Full Employment. University of Birmingham. (Mimeographed.)

———. (1953). Absence and labour turnover in a changing economic climate. Occupational Psychology, 27, 69-70.

———. (1959). Voluntary absence from work. International Labour Review, 79, 109-140.

———. (1974). A new approach to the analysis of absence from work. Industrial Relations Journal, 5, 4-21.

Best, F., and B. S. Stern (1977). Education, work and leisure: Must they come in that order? Monthly Labor Review, 100, no. 7 (July), 3-9.

Blackler, F. H. M., and C. A. Brown (1975). The impending crisis in job redesign. Occupational Psychology, 48, 185-193.

Blood, M. R. (1971). The validity of importance. Journal of Applied Psychology, 55, 487-488.

Brayfield, A. H., and W. H. Crockett (1955). Employee attitudes and employee performance. Psychological Bulletin, 52, 396-424.

Broadbent, D. E. (1980). The minimization of models. In A. J. Chapman and D. M. Jones (eds.), Models of Man. Leicester: British Psychological Society.

Brodman, K., and L. P. Hellman (1947). The relation of group morale to the incidence and duration of medical incapacity in industry. Psychosomatic Medicine, 9, 381-385.

Burke, R. J., and D. S. Wilcox (1972). Absenteeism and turnover among female telephone operators. Personnel Psychology, 25, 639-648.

Butler, E. A., and B. J. Hay (1977). The passionate statistician: A computerized record of nursing sickness and absence 2. Nursing Times 73, 153-156.

Buzzard, R. B. (1954). Attendance and absence in industry: The nature of the evidence. British Journal of Sociology, 5, 238-252.

Buzzard, R. B., and F. D. K. Liddell (1958). Coal-miners attendance at work. Medical Research Memorandum no. 3. National Coal Board Medical Service.

Buzzard, R. B., and W. J. Shaw (1952). An analysis of absence under a scheme of paid sick leave. British Journal of Industrial Medicine, 9, 282-295.

Campbell, D. T., and D. W. Fiske (1959). Convergent and discriminant validation by the multitrait-multimethod matrix. Psychological Bulletin, 56, 81-105.

Castle, P. F. C. (1956). Accidents, absence and withdrawal from the work situation. Human Relations, 9, 223-233.

Chadwick-Jones, J. K. (1969). Automation and Behaviour: A Social Psychological Study. London and New York: Wiley.

——. (1976). Social Exchange Theory: Its Structure and Influence in Social Psychology. New York: Academic Press.

——. (1978). Absence Measures and Trends in a Banking Organization. Ottawa: Report to Canada Labour.

——. (1980). Absenteeism in the Canadian Context. Labour Canada Monograph. Ottawa: Department of Labour.

——. (1981). Five New Absence Measures. Ottawa: Report to Canada Labour.

Chadwick-Jones, J. K., C. A. Brown, N. Nicholson, and C. Sheppard (1971). Absence measures: Their reliability and stability in an industrial setting. Personnel Psychology, 24, 463-470.

Chadwick-Jones, J. K., C. A. Brown, and N. Nicholson (1973a). Absence from work: Its meaning, measurement and control. International Review of Applied Psychology, *22*, 137–155.

——. (1973b). A-type and B-type absence: Empirical trends for women employees. Occupational Psychology, *47*, 75–80.

Clark, J. (1975) Time out? London, Royal College of Nursing.

Clark, W. (1971). How to cut absenteeism and turnover. Administrative Management Society Report, March, 64–65.

Cleland, S. (1955). The Influence of Plant Size on Industrial Relations. Princeton, N.J.: Industrial Relations Section, Department of Economics and Sociology, Princeton University.

Cohen, A. R., and H. Gadon (1978). Alternative Work Schedules: Integrating Individual and Organizational Needs. Reading, Mass.: Addison-Wesley.

Cooper, R., and R. L. Payne (1965). Age and absence: A longitudinal study in three firms. Occupational Psychology, *39*, 31–35.

Cornwall, C. J., and P. A. B. Raffle (1961). Sickness absence of women bus conductors in London Transport (1953–1957). British Journal of Industrial Medicine, *18*, 197–212.

Costello, T. W. (1975). The industrial psychologist looks at absenteeism. In S. F. Yolles, P. A. Carone, and L. W. Krinsky (eds.), Absenteeism in Industry. Springfield, Ill.: Charles C. Thomas.

Cross, D. (1973). The worker opinion survey: A measure of shop-floor satisfaction. Occupational Psychology, *47*, 193–208.

Davis, L. E., and A. B. Cherns (eds.) (1975). The Quality of Working Life, vol. I, Problems, Prospects and the State of the Art. New York: Free Press.

de la Mare. G., and Sergean R. (1961) Two methods of studying changes in absence with age. Occupational Psychology, *35*, 245–252.

Denerley, R. A. (1952). Some effects of paid sick leave on sickness absence. British Journal of Industrial Medicine, *9*, 275–281.

Denett, B. (1978). How to minimize malingering. Personnel Management, May, 30–32.

Ferguson, D. (1972). Some characteristics of repeated sickness absence. British Journal of Industrial Medicine, *29*, 420–431.

Fox, A. (1976). The meaning of work. In People and Work, block 3, unit 6. Milton Keynes: Open University Press.

Fox, J. B., and J. F. Scott (1943). Absenteeism: Management's problem. Business Research Studies no. 29, 30. Cambridge, Mass.: Harvard Business School, Division of Research.

Fraser, R. (1947). The incidence of neurosis among factory workers. M.R.C. Industrial Health Research Board Report no. 90. London: HMSO.

Froggatt, P. (1970a). Short-term absence from industry: I. Literature, definitions, data, and the effect of age and length of service. British Journal of Industrial Medicine, *27*, 199–210.

——. (1970b). Short-term absence from industry: II. Temporal variation and inter-association with other recorded factors. Ibid., 211–224.

——. (1970c). Short-term absence from industry: III. The inference of "proneness" and a search for causes. Ibid., 297–312.

Gadourek, I. (1965). Absences and Well-Being of Workers. Assen, Netherlands: Van Gorcum.

Gary, A. L. (1971). Industrial absenteeism: An evaluation of three methods of treatment. Personnel Journal, May, 352–353.

Gaudet, F. J. (1963). Solving the Problems of Employee Absence. New York: American Management Association.

Gerstenfeld, A. (1969). Employee absenteeism: New insights. Business Horizons, October, 51–57.

Gibson, J. O. (1966). Toward a conceptualization of absence behaviour of personnel in organizations. Administrative Science Quarterly, *2*, 107–133.

Globerson, S., and P. J. Nagarvala (1974). Unexplained absenteeism: A simulation approach. Washington, D.C.: Winter Simulation Conference Annual Proceedings, 54–55.

Goffman, E. (1968). Asylums. Harmondsworth: Penguin Books.

Gordon, C., A. R. Emerson, and D. S. Pugh (1959). Patterns of sickness absence in a railway population. British Journal of Industrial Medicine, *16*, 230–244.

Grossman, E. (1978). Incentives to reduce absenteeism. Dimensions in Health Service, December, 26–27.

Hackman, J. R., and E. E. Lawler (1971). Employee reactions to job characteristics. Journal of Applied Psychology Monograph, 55, 259–286.

Hammer, T. H., and J. Landau (1981). Methodological issues in the use of absentee data. Journal of Applied Psychology, 66, 574–581.

Harding, F. D., and R. A. Bottenberg (1961). Effect of personal characteristics on relationships between attitudes and job performance. Journal of Applied Psychology, 45, 428–430.

Hedges, J. N. (1973). Absence from work—a look at some national data. Monthly Labour Review, July, 24–31.

——. (1975). Unscheduled absence from work—an update. Monthly Labour Review, August, 36–39.

——. (1977). Absence from work—measuring the hours lost. Monthly Labour Review, October, 16–23.

Heron, A. (1960). Ageing and employment. In R. S. F. Schilling (ed.), Modern Trends in Occupational Health. London: Butterworth.

Herzberg, F., B. Mausner, R. O. Peterson, and D. F. Capwell (1957). Job Attitudes: Review of Research and Opinion. Pittsburgh: Psychological Service of Pittsburgh.

Hewitt, D., and J. Parfit (1953). A note on working morale and size of group. Occupational Psychology, 17, 38–42.

Hill, J. M. M., and E. L. Trist (1953). A consideration of industrial accidents as a means of withdrawal from the work situation. Human Relations, 6, 357–380.

——. (1955). Changes in accidents and other absences with length of service. Human Relations, 8, 121–152.

——. (1962). Industrial Accidents, Sickness and Other Absences. Tavistock Pamphlet no. 4. London: Tavistock Publications.

Hinrichs, J. R. (1968). A replicated study of job satisfaction dimensions. Personnel Psychology, 21, 479–503.

Huse, E. F., and E. K. Taylor (1962). The reliability of absence measures. Journal of Applied Psychology, 46, 159–160.

Indik, B. P. (1963). Some effects of organisational size on member attitudes and behaviour. Human Relations, 16, 369–384.

Ingham, G. K. (1970). Size of Industrial Organisation and Worker Behaviour. London: Cambridge University Press.

Isambert-Jamati, V. (1962). Absenteeism among women workers in industry. International Labour Review, *85*, 248–261.

Jardillier, P. (1962). Study of 14 factors affecting industrial absenteeism. Travail Humaine, *25*, 107–116.

Johns, G. (1978). Attitudinal and non-attitudinal predictors of two forms of absence from work. Organizational Behavior and Human Performance, *22*, 431–444.

Jones, R. M. (1971). Absenteeism. Manpower Papers no. 4. London: HMSO, Department of Employment.

Katz, D., and H. Hyman (1947). Industrial morale and public opinion methods. International Journal of Opinion and Attitude Research, *1*, 13–30.

Kerr, W. A., G. J. Koppelmeier, and J. J. Sullivan (1951). Absenteeism, turnover and morale in a metals fabrication factory. Occupational Psychology, *25*, 50–55.

Kilbridge, M. D. (1961). Turnover, absence, and transfer rates as indicators of employee dissatisfaction with repetitive work. Industrial and Labour Relations Review, *15*, 21–32.

Knox, J. B. (1961). Absenteeism and turnover in an Argentine factory. American Sociological Review, *26*, 424–428.

Kornhauser, A. W., and A. A. Sharp (1932). Employee attitude: Suggestions from a study in a factory. Personnel Journal, *10*, 393–404.

Lawler, E. E., and J. R. Hackman (1969). Impact of employee participation in the development of pay incentive plans: A field experiment. Journal of Applied Psychology, *53*, 467–471.

Lawler, E. E., and H. W. Porter (1967). Antecedent attitudes and effective managerial performance. Organisational Behaviour and Human Performance, *2*, 122–142.

Levin, J. (1970). Absenteeism and lateness: How much are they costing your firm? Office Administration, *16*, 34–35.

Liddell, F. D. K. (1954). The measurement of daily variations in absence. Applied Statistics, *3*, 104–111.

Lokander, S. (1962). Sick absence in a Swedish company: A socio-medical study. Acta Medica Scandinavica, *171*, supp. 377.

Lundquist, A. (1959). Absenteeism and job turnover as a consequence of unfavorable job adjustment. Acta Sociologica, *3*, 119-131.

Lyons, T. F. (1972). Turnover and absenteeism: A review of the relationships and shared correlates. Personnel Psychology, *25*, 271-281.

Mackenzie, B. D. (1977). Behaviourism and the Limits of Scientific Method. Atlantic Highlands, N.J.: Humanities Press.

Mann, F. C., and H. Baumgartel (1952). Absences and Employee Attitudes in an Electric Power Company. Human Relations Program series 1, Report no. 2. Ann Arbor: Institute for Social Research, University of Michigan.

Mann, F. C., B. P. Indik, and V. H. Vroom (1963). The Productivity of Work Groups. Ann Arbor: Institute for Social Research, University of Michigan.

Marcuse, H. (1972). Counter-revolution and Revolt. London: Allen Lane/The Penguin Press.

Martin, J. (1971). Some aspects of absence in a light engineering factory. Occupational Psychology, *45*, 77-89.

Mauss, M. (1954). The Gift. Glencoe, Ill.: Free Press.

Metzner, H., and F. C. Mann (1953). Employee attitudes and absences. Personnel Psychology, *6*, 467-485.

Mikalachki, A. (1975). The effects of job design on turnover, absenteeism and health. Industrial Relations, *30*, 377-389.

Mikalachki, A., and D. C. Chapple (1977). Absenteeism and overtime: Double jeopardy. Industrial Relations, *32*, 532-545.

Mikes, P. S., and C. L. Hulin (1968). Use of importance as a weighting component of job satisfaction. Journal of Applied Psychology, *52*, 394-398.

Mirvis, P. H., and E. E. Lawler (1977). Measuring the financial impact of employee attitudes. Journal of Applied Psychology, *62*, 1-8.

Mobley, W. H., and E. A. Locke (1970). The relationship of value importance to satisfaction. Organisational Behaviour and Human Performance, *5*, 463-483.

Moos, S. (1951). The statistics of absenteeism in coal mining. Manchester School of Economic and Social Studies, *19*, 89-108.

Morgan, L. G., and J. B. Herman (1976). Perceived consequences of absenteeism. Journal of Applied Psychology, 61, 738–742.

Muchinsky, P. M. (1977). Employee absenteeism: A review of the literature. Journal of Vocational Behavior, 10, 316–340.

Naylor, J. C., R. D. Pritchard, and D. R. Ilgen (1980). A Theory of Behavior in Organizations. New York: Academic Press.

Newman, J. E. (1974). Predicting absenteeism and turnover: A field comparison of Fishbein's model and traditional job attitude measures. Journal of Applied Psychology, 59, 610–615.

Nicholson, N., C. A. Brown, and J. K. Chadwick-Jones (1976). Absence from work and job satisfaction. Journal of Applied Psychology, 61, 728–737.

——. (1977). Absence from work and personal characteristics. Journal of Applied Psychology, 62, 319–327.

Nicholson, N., T. D. Wall, and J. Lischeron (1977). The predictability of absence and propensity to leave from employees' job satisfactions and attitudes towards influence in decision-making. Human Relations, 30, 499–514.

Nickson, M. (1972) Absentees—off work for health reasons. Canada 1970. Notes on Labour Statistics, Statistics Canada (Catalogue 72–207 Annual). Ottawa, Information Canada.

Noland, E. W. (1945) Worker attitudes and industrial absenteeism—a statistical approach. American Sociological Review, 10, 503–510.

Nord, W. (1970). Improving attendance through rewards. Personnel Administration, November, 37–41.

Nova Scotia Department of Labour (1976). Labour Turnover and Absenteeism in Nova Scotia's Manufacturing Industries 1974. Economics and Research Division, Halifax.

Office of Population Censuses and Surveys (1973). General Household Survey: Introductory Report. London: OPCS Social Survey Division, HMSO.

Patchen, M. (1960). Absence and employee feelings about fair treatment. Personnel Psychology, 13, 349–360.

Payne, R. L., S. Fineman, and T. D. Wall (1975). Organisational climate and job satisfaction: A conceptual systhesis. In Organisational Behaviour and Human Performance, 16, 45–62.

Plummer, N. (1960). Absenteeism in industry. Advanced Management, 25, 21–24.

Pocock, S. J. (1973). Relationship between sickness absence and length of service. British Journal of Industrial Medicine, *30*, 64–70.

Porter, L. W., and R. M. Steers (1973). Organisational, work, and personal factors in employee turnover and absenteeism. Psychological Bulletin, *80*, 151–176.

Portis, B., and J. Bertrand (1978). Managing turnover and absenteeism. Canadian Personnel and Industrial Relations Journal, 31–35.

Revans, R. W. (1960). Morale and the size of the working group. In R. S. F. Schilling (ed.), Modern Trends in Occupational Health. London: Butterworth.

Robertson, G., and J. Humphreys (1978). Labour Turnover and Absenteeism in Selected Industries: Northwestern Ontario and Ontario. Toronto: Ontario Ministry of Labour.

Sanderson, G. F. (1979). Absenteeism, its extent, causes and costs. Ottawa: Canadian International Development Agency. (Unpublished Paper.)

Scheflen, K. C., E. E. Lawler, and J. R. Hackman (1971). Long-term impact of employee participation in the development of pay incentive plans: A field experiment revisited. Journal of Applied Psychology, *55*, 182–186.

Schenet, N. G. (1945). An analysis of absenteeism in one war plant. Journal of Applied Psychology, *19*, 27–39.

Scherba, J., and L. Smith (1973). Computerization of absentee control programs. Personnel Journal, May, 367–372.

Schwartz, B. (1974). Waiting, exchange and power: The distribution of time in social systems. American Journal of Sociology, *79*, 841–870.

Seatter, W. C. (1961). More effective control of absenteeism. Personnel, *38*, 16–29.

Simpson, J. (1962). Sickness absence in teachers. British Journal of Industrial Medicine, *19*, 110–115.

Smith, P. C., L. M. Kendall, and C. L. Hulin (1969). The Measurement of Satisfaction in Work and Retirement: A Strategy for the Study of Attitudes. Chicago: Rand McNally.

Steers, R. M., and S. R. Rhodes (1978). Major influences on employee attendance: A process model. Journal of Applied Psychology, *63*, 391–407.

Sternhagen, C. J. (1969). Medicine's role in reducing absenteeism. Personnel, November–December, 28–31.

Talachi, S. (1960). Organisation size, individual attitudes and behaviour: An Empirical study. Administrative Science Quarterly, 5, 398–420.

Taylor, P. J. (1968). Sickness absence resistance. Transactions of the Society of Occupational Medicine, 18, 96–100.

——. (1974). Sickness absence: Facts and misconceptions. Journal of the Royal College of Physicians London, 8, 315–334.

Thibault, A. (1967). Comparative examination of male and female absenteeism and turnover in the labour force. Royal Commission on the Status of Women in Canada. (Unpublished Study.)

U.S. Bureau of National Affairs (1974). Employee absenteeism and turnover. Personnel Policies Forum, no. 106, May 1–46.

U.S. Department of Labor (1951). Suggestions for control of turnover and absenteeism. Washington, D.C.

——. (1972). Suggestions for control of turnover and absenteeism. Washington, D.C.

Van Zelst, R. H., and W. A. Kerr (1953). Workers' attitudes toward merit rating. Personnal Psychology, 6, 159–172.

Vroom, V. H. (1962). Ego-involvement, job satisfaction, and job performance. Personnel Psychology, 15, 159–177.

——. (1964). Work and Motivation. New York: Wiley.

Walker, K. (1947). The application of the J-curve hypothesis of conforming behavior to industrial absenteeism. Journal of Social Psychology, 25, 207–216.

Warr, P. B., and T. Routledge (1969). An opinion scale for the study of managers' job satisfaction. Occupational Psychology, 43, 95–109.

Waters, L. K., and D. Roach (1971). Relationship between job attitudes and two forms of withdrawal from the work situation. Journal of Applied Psychology, 55, 92–94.

——. (1973). Job attitudes as predictors of termination and absenteeism: Consistency over time and across organisational levels. Journal of Applied Psychology, 57, 341–342.

White, B. L. (1960). Job attitudes, absence from work and labour turnover. Personnel Practice Bulletin, 16, 18–23.

Williams, A., B. Livy, R. Silverstone, and P. Adams (1979). Factors associated with labour turnover among ancillary staff in two London hospitals. Journal of Occupational Psychology, *52*, 1–16.

Yolles, S. F., P. A. Carone, and L. W. Krinsky (1975). Absenteeism in Industry. Springfield, Ill.: Charles C. Thomas.

INDEX

ABOUT THE AUTHORS

JOHN CHADWICK-JONES, Ph.D., D.Sc., Professor of Psychology, Saint Mary's University, Halifax, Canada, was formerly Director of the Occupational Psychology Research Unit, Cardiff University, Wales, and Reader in Social Psychology at The Flinders University of South Australia. During 1980–81 he was Canada S.S.H.R.C. Fellow at St. Edmund Hall, University of Oxford, and at Darwin College, University of Cambridge. He is author of *Automation and Behaviour: A Social Psychological Study* (1969) and *Social Exchange Theory: Its Structure and Influence in Social Psychology* (1976), and coauthor of *Brain, Environment and Social Psychology* (1979).

COLIN BROWN, Ph.D., of the Department of Behaviour in Organizations, Lancaster University, England, was formerly Research Assistant in the Occupational Psychology Research Unit, Cardiff University, Wales. He is coauthor of the *Access Case Book* (1976), *Job Redesign and Management Control* (1978), and *Whatever Happened to Shell's New Philosophy of Management?* (1980).

NIGEL NICHOLSON, Ph.D., Senior Research Fellow in the Medical Research Council Social and Applied Psychology Unit of Sheffield University, England, was formerly Research Assistant in the Occupational Psychology Research Unit, Cardiff University, Wales. During 1980–81 he was Visiting Associate Professor, Department of Business Administration, University of Illinois at Urbana-Champaign. He is coauthor of *Developing Employee Relations* (1978), *The Dynamics of White-Collar Unionism* (1981), and *Steel Strike* (in press), and coeditor of *Essays in the Theory and Practice of Organizational Psychology* (1981).